SALES
EFFECTIVENESS
TRAINING

CARL D. ZAISS AND THOMAS GORDON, PH.D.

SALES
EFFECTIVENESS
TRAINING

THE BREAKTHROUGH METHOD TO BECOME
PARTNERS WITH YOUR CUSTOMERS

A DUTTON BOOK

DUTTON

Published by the Penguin Group
Penguin Books USA Inc., 375 Hudson Street, New York, New York 10014, U.S.A.
Penguin Books Ltd, 27 Wrights Lane, London W8 5TZ, England
Penguin Books Australia Ltd, Ringwood, Victoria, Australia
Penguin Books Canada Ltd, 10 Alcorn Avenue, Toronto, Ontario, Canada M4V 3B2
Penguin Books (N.Z.) Ltd, 182–190 Wairau Road, Auckland 10, New Zealand

Penguin Books Ltd, Registered Offices:
Harmondsworth, Middlesex, England

First published by Dutton, an imprint of Dutton Signet,
a division of Penguin Books USA Inc.
Distributed in Canada by McClelland & Stewart Inc.

First Printing, October, 1993
1 3 5 7 9 10 8 6 4 2

 REGISTERED TRADEMARK—MARCA REGISTRADA

Library of Congress Cataloging-in-Publication Data

Zaiss, Carl D.
Sales effectiveness training : the breakthrough method to become partners with your
customers / Carl D. Zaiss and Thomas Gordon.
p. cm.
ISBN 0-525-93676-9
1. Selling. 2. Sales personnel—Training of. 3. Interpersonal relations.
4. Customer relations. 5. Selling—Psychological aspects.
I. Gordon, Thomas, 1918- . II. Title.
HF5438.25.Z34 1993
658.85—dc20   93-4486
                                                                                CIP

Printed in the United States of America
Set in Copperplate 29bc and Century Expanded

Designed by Steven N. Stathakis

THIS BOOK IS DEDICATED TO OUR FAMILIES
AND LOVED ONES.

C O N T E N T S

CONTENTS

ACKNOWLEDGMENTS

Many people have contributed in different ways to our work together and to this book. To acknowledge individuals in this form is our way of expressing our appreciation and recognizing the contributions they have made.

First, to Alex Kerr and Michael Bender for their courage and conviction. They are true pioneers in the exploration of the new model of selling. Both searched for new answers to the challenges of selling rather than relying on the status quo—the easy way out. Their commitments to both the success of their organizations and their own beliefs about selling led them to our Synergistic Selling course. From our work with Alex and Michael, we learned a great deal that furthered our own discovery process. We would also like to thank the thousands of individuals who have participated in the Synergistic Selling program. Their feedback provided constant reassurance that we were on the right path. Their successes fueled our own commitment to the new model, and their breakdowns showed us what was missing to complete the transformation.

At Penguin USA, we wish to thank Alexia Dorszynski and Arnold Dolin for their initial support of the project, John Paine for his brilliant editing of the first manuscript, and Deb Brody for her ongoing partnership and her commitment to our vision.

And a special note of thanks from Carl Zaiss to the following:

To Walt and Fran Johnson for their continuous love and support.

To Sally Skinner and Patrick Sobota for introducing me to Tom Gordon's work.

To Ann Bauer, David and Nancy Grundman, Chuck Hitzemann, Deborah Naish, Nathan Rosenberg, John Smith, and Paul Spitler for their always insightful conversations and stimulating support during the writing of the manuscript.

To Sheryl Sneag, whose partnership contributed in major ways to the foundation and early development of the manuscript and to Denyse Raskin for her help with the finishing touches.

A personal note of appreciation to Alison Armstrong. Her ongoing coaching and her commitment to personal development have helped me move beyond my own boundaries of success.

Thanks to all of you.

PURPOSE

The purpose of this book is to provide you, the reader, with a new set of skills and concepts that will enable you to break through the boundaries of traditional selling and create *extraordinary* results in your sales performance.

This book represents a breakthrough in the field of selling. *The American Heritage Dictionary* defines *breakthrough* as "a major achievement or success that permits further progress." Our commitment is to provide a model that allows you to move beyond what is usual, normal, or customary. The kind of leap we are dedicated to encompasses a shift to results that are extraordinary.

We hope you will find this book a valuable key to unlocking the gates to higher possibilities in your sales career.

SALES
EFFECTIVENESS
TRAINING

TWO VIEWS OF SALES

CARL ZAISS: A PROFESSIONAL SALESPERSON'S LOOK AT SALES

For more than twenty-five years, I have been involved with sales in many different forms. This includes retail sales during college, various sales positions throughout my career in the hotel business, and, since 1982, selling my own training programs and consulting services, in addition to training other salespeople. This background has provided me the opportunities to experience personally, and explore with others, the attitudes and behaviors essential for success in selling. Everywhere I go, I find salespeople searching for new answers to meet the challenges of an ever changing marketplace.

The traditional approach to sales simply doesn't work anymore. Most salespeople are taught skills and techniques that are actually detrimental to their success. Particularly harmful are attempts to control another person. Taught in most sales training, this desire to control is counterproductive to a salesperson's basic responsibility—establishing a rapport with the buyer that allows for an open exchange of information.

It is time that we come to a higher level of understanding about the complexity of the seller-buyer relationship. This change does not mean "a little better, a little different," but rather a significant change in the way we perceive the seller-buyer relationship, even a transformation. To do this, we must first recognize the limitations of the existing model and break out of the shells of traditional thinking and behavior. Then we must develop new skills that provide the foundation for the change.

The motivation for this transformation must come from *you*. It cannot be mandated by others in your organization. To help you get started, let me tell you some of my experiences in sales and why I came to feel trapped. Then you can determine what you would like to do to enhance your success and satisfaction from sales.

My first true sales job was as a child when I sold candy to raise money for Little League baseball. A box of Russell Stover chocolates sold for a buck back then, and the incentive for the most sales was a baseball jacket. To ensure that the goal was met, a quota was established for each ballplayer.

Every year I started out excited. I could just see myself wearing the new jacket. My parents spent hours driving me around to various neighborhoods. Eventually, though, knocking on strange doors and being told no would get to me, and my enthusiasm would wane. Many times my parents bought the last few boxes so my quota would be met.

Before long the candy drive became a yearly obligation that I resented. The people whose homes I visited became the adversaries—obstacles on my path. This attitude, as salespeople well know, eliminated any chance of success. I decided that I wasn't good at selling and that I didn't like it.

After college, when I entered the hotel business, I soon realized that a few years in sales would advance my career, so I made the transition to selling. And guess what? I still didn't like it. That should not be surprising considering the perceptions I had already developed about sales and my chances for success. As before, the hours of cold calling and prospecting for business eventually took their toll. Even the glamorous sales trips, cocktail parties, conventions, and trade shows became all work and no fun. I felt that I was always on stage, playing a role. I looked forward to the end of the day, when I could take off my mask.

And there were other reasons for my frustrations, reasons I'm sure other salespeople will relate to. First of all, selling seemed to be a chess game between the buyer and me—someone had to win and someone had to lose. Whatever tactics I needed to win, I used to beat the other guy.

Second, for years top management did not appreciate or support the sales function. If business was up, they cited the economy or the fine reputation for service the hotel had built. Only when business was down did they notice the sales department. After all, a good salesperson should overcome whatever obstacles were in the way to bringing in business.

Third, many times I had more difficulty with the support departments delivering what was sold than I did with my clients. The stress of getting the business was nothing compared to that of keeping it.

Finally, as a salesperson, I didn't see any way to get my needs met. It seemed to me that the only way to get and keep customers was to subordinate my needs. That left me feeling frustrated and resentful, leaving me very little satisfaction from my job.

I read books and I attended training programs, but they didn't fit my needs. They all taught control, manipulation, and deceit. If that's what selling was, what did that make me?

Throughout my career, discussions with other salespeople confirmed my beliefs. I not only heard them voice similar frustrations, but I watched the heavy turnover in sales departments take its toll. Something was wrong with the system.

In 1982, I left the hotel business to form my own training and consulting organization. I was committed to finding answers to the problems I had experienced in the workplace and then to sharing that information with others. I began to search for answers to some basic questions. Can a person succeed in sales while feeling true to himself? Does trying so hard to close a sale strain the seller-buyer relationship in the long run? Can a win-win outcome be created in the seller-buyer relationship?

In my search, I met Dr. Thomas Gordon, a pioneer in interpersonal-skills training. I had personally experienced the benefits of his Parent Effectiveness Training (P.E.T.) and Leader Effectiveness Training (L.E.T.) books and training courses. In both I discovered a set of skills and concepts that enabled me to build and maintain mutually beneficial relationships with my family, friends, and colleagues at work. As our relationship developed, Tom and I spent many hours discussing how his model applies to the seller-buyer relationship.

As a result of these discussions and our shared belief that there had to be a better way, we collaborated on the development of Synergistic Selling, a significant step beyond traditional sales training. This course was, and still is, the leading edge in sales training.

Since that time, I have taught Synergistic Selling throughout the United States, Canada, and Europe to organizations of all sizes, from small entrepreneurial ventures to such large corporations as General Motors. Through this experience, I have discovered that I was not alone in my early perceptions and frustrations regarding sales. Everywhere I go, I meet salespeople and sales managers disenchanted with the traditional model of selling. They're eager to hear a new way, yet uncomfortable with the change this transformation represents.

During the seminars I lead, I break my group in half and assign one group to be the sellers, the other the buyers. I then ask the buyers to describe sellers. The most common terms and phrases they use are *liars, cheats, pushy, arrogant, not concerned about the buyers, once you buy you never see them again.* But turnabout is fair play, so I ask the sellers to describe buyers. They are *dishonest, stubborn, ignorant, demanding, play both ends against the middle, not open to new ideas.* The traditional model of sales pits the seller against the buyer.

Sales managers and others in the organization, in most cases unknowingly, perpetuate the traditional model of the seller-buyer relationship. Their rules have a lot of influence over salespeople—much more than any statements of ethics and purpose printed, promoted, and distributed throughout the organization. The very language used to describe the seller-buyer relationship, the factors determining salespeople's rewards, the training they receive, and management's priorities in tough situations—all reinforce the traditional model of the adversarial seller-buyer relationship.

What I'm saying is that the entire profession of sales needs an overhaul. The traditional model is simply too confining and inadequate for today's business world. What's needed is a transformation.

The relationship blueprint developed by Tom Gordon is the key to this necessary overhaul of the seller-buyer relationship. *Sales Effectiveness Training* reflects my commitment to the skills I have mastered and in turn taught others.

This book will provide you the same opportunity to move beyond existing preconditioned beliefs and behavior models and create more effective, potent, and satisfying relationships as you expand into new success in selling.

TOM GORDON: A PSYCHOLOGIST'S LOOK AT SALES

I became interested in sales in the late 1950s, soon after I had started my career as an organizational consultant specializing in human relations. I worked with clients to solve such problems as How do you select salespeople who will be successful? What are the best methods for training salespeople? How do you reduce turnover of salespeople? How do you motivate another person to buy what you have to sell?

The last problem interested me the most and led me to focus directly on this highly complex process. At that time, little research shed light on what goes on when a seller influences a buyer. However, my training in psychology had exposed me to research studies that examined the influence process in other relationships—boss-subordinate, parent-child, and counselor-client. All of these relationships feature one person trying to influence someone else to do something that person may not want to do. Could these findings be applied to the seller-buyer relationship? Certainly, we have to do some selling in all our relationships.

One of my first steps was to identify five requirements of a successful selling process:

1. The salesperson must discover what the buyer's needs are and try to meet them.
2. The buyer must feel that the salesperson is transparently real, believable, and trustworthy.
3. The buyer must be given the opportunity to voice his objections, doubts, and fears, and have them *accepted* by the seller.
4. The buyer must feel he has made a decision freely without being pushed or manipulated.
5. The buyer must feel that the salesperson is a friend, a partner, a counselor.

Intrigued, I began applying these principles in my work with the sales departments of several clients: Forest E. Olson, then the largest real estate firm in Los Angeles; Forest Lawn, a prestigious mortuary and funeral organization; and Avery Label, a pioneer in the field of pressure label products. Training salespeople to build and maintain such relationships with customers, I believed, should be similar to my work training professional counselors at the University of Chicago from 1949 to 1954. In a speech I gave to the national convention of the Sales Executives Club in 1958, entitled

"Should Salesmen Learn the Counselor's Art of Listening?" I predicted: "A sales training program designed like training for effective counselors would equip salespeople with some of the same skills, attitudes and sensitivities as trained counselors. To my way of thinking it would not be an inaccurate way of describing the role of a successful salesperson as that of a *counselor for his customers.*"

In another speech a year later, entitled "Person-Centered Sales Training," I identified four components of an effective training program for salespeople.

1. *Spontaneity training:* Teach salespeople to behave spontaneously, to get out of learned "roles," to drop their "acts," to feel safe just being their real selves; to be flexible, to avoid memorized sales pitches.
2. *Listening training:* Teach salespeople to put less emphasis on persuading buyers and more on listening to buyers; teach an effective counselor's principal skill— empathic Active Listening. This skill communicates to a prospective buyer or long-term customer: "I want to hear your problems and needs. I want to hear and accept your feelings, whatever they may be—doubt, reluctance, uncertainty, indecisiveness."
3. *Attitude training:* Sensitize salespeople to the complexities of human behavior—people's unpredictability; their almost universal resistance to change; their need to make their own decisions; and their distrust of efforts to push or manipulate them.
4. *Impact training:* Provide the opportunity for salespeople to learn what kind of impact their communication has on other people. Create a climate in a group of trainees that encourages sharing how each one comes across to the others.

I concluded this speech on sales training by predicting: "I am convinced that if we train salespeople as persons, and if we later supervise them as persons, they will become skilled in establishing effective personal relations with their customers, and we will be contributing to making selling more of a profession in which its members feel a sense of personal dignity, pride and self-respect."

Not until twenty years after that prediction did my organization, Effectiveness Training, enter the sales-training market with its program SalesTech. During those two decades, we concentrated our efforts first on marketing a training program for parents, called Parent Effectiveness Training (P.E.T.). That program, launched in 1962, was the first to teach parents the skills required to build and maintain mutually satisfying relationships with children of all ages. It was an immediate success. By 1992, our cadre of several thousand specially trained and authorized P.E.T. instructors had taught over a million parents in thirty-one countries throughout the world.

In the early 1970s, we launched Teacher Effectiveness Training (T.E.T.), a program that pioneered teaching interpersonal skills to school teachers. Soon after that, we developed Leader Effectiveness Training (L.E.T.), a course for supervisors, managers, and executives in organizations. This program was one of the first to teach the skills required for participative management, employee involvement in decision making, and team building.

The success of each of these Effectiveness Training courses convinced me that we had identified the critical skills for building a special kind of person-to-person relationship. First, it was mutually satisfying because through it both persons satisfied their needs. Second, it did not involve power-based control or manipulation. Third, the relationship endured because it felt "fair" to both persons.

When we developed and began marketing our first sales-training program, SalesTech, in the early 1980s, we were not surprised that salespeople quickly learned these same skills and successfully used them to develop more mutually satisfying and collaborative relationships with their buyers and customers.

Effectiveness Training is now marketing its second sales-training program, Synergistic Selling. It focuses on (1) enhancing the relationship between seller and buyer; (2) teaching the seller how to help buyers through the stages of buying; and (3) teaching salespeople the skills for making sure their own needs are met in relationships with customers.

This book will give readers a deeper understanding of Synergistic Selling and the remarkable benefits to be derived from using it—whether selling services and products to customers or selling your ideas to associates at work. Many of the issues covered in this book are derived from the extensive experience of co-author Carl Zaiss. He has been a sales manager, a sales trainer, as well as a salesperson, and he is a strong advocate for a new model of selling, along with a new model for managing salespeople. Together, Carl and I collaborated on the development of the Synergistic Selling course, building from the basic systems in other Effectiveness Training programs.

In this book, we will show why successful seller-buyer partnerships have become more necessary in our business environment. Trying to manipulate or control customers is an out-of-date process that must be replaced by win-win (or no-lose) relationships—based on mutually satisfying trust and respect for the needs of both parties. This sort of partnership has a better chance of lasting.

The book also stresses the necessity of the salesperson's organization using the new model to support Synergistic Selling. We look critically at the way sales managers relate to salespeople, and we evaluate the conventional approach to sales training.

Above all, Synergistic Selling, as I predicted in that speech over three decades ago, will make sales a more valued profession in which its members feel a sense of personal dignity, pride, and self-respect.

WHY THE TRADITIONAL

SALES MODEL

DOESN'T WORK

The era of the one-night stand is gone. . . . The sale merely consummates the courtship, at which time the marriage begins.

—THEODORE LEVITT

It is time for a major breakthrough in the profession of selling. Today's complex business climate makes the traditional model of selling obsolete. To keep pace with the needs of an ever-changing business environment, success in selling today requires a radical departure from conventional thinking.

In a 1983 *Harvard Business Review* article, Theodore Levitt, then head of the marketing area at the Harvard Business School, said: "As our economy becomes more service- and technology-oriented, the dynamics of the sales process will change. The ongoing nature of services and the ongoing complexity of technology will increasingly necessitate lengthy and involved relationships between buyers and sellers. Thus, the seller's focus will need to shift from merely landing sales to ensuring buyer satisfaction after the purchase."

At the time Levitt's article was written, dramatic shifts were occurring in the business environment that would set the stage for the balance of the 1980s. If anything, these changes have accelerated in the early 1990s, making Levitt's prophecy more accurate. As a result, selling today requires a totally new set of skills. Rather than "closing" skills, salespeople need to acquire "relationship management" skills.

Besides increased technological complexity, there are several other factors calling forth this shift. First, increased competition in almost every segment of the economy increases the need for stronger customer loyalty in the form of long-term relationships. Second, the increased cost of bringing in new business versus the lower cost of keeping satisfied customers makes the development of longer-term customers even more economically desirable. Finally, the "quality" movement demands closer partnerships between buyers and sellers. W. Edwards Deming, referred to by many as the father of the quality movement, stresses this in his fourteen points for quality management. He emphasizes the value of working with a single source supplier to improve the supplier's quality and lower its costs, thereby cultivating a long-term relationship in which both will profit.

Furthermore, as sales becomes more complex, stronger relationships with others involved with the delivery of products and services are required as well. A salesperson must communicate with an increasingly important interdependent network of people instrumental to his success. Within organizations, the growing number of departments involved with customer service and customer support demands a greater emphasis on interdepartmental communication. And independent salespeople have a similar and just as complex network of people involved with their sales process. A salesperson, in this trend, is a leader who must coordinate the efforts of a team of people in order to deliver quality products and services to the customer.

Both buyers and sellers also want a change in the relationship. Today's buyer is more sensitive to traditional sales techniques and is looking for someone to step out of the typical salesperson's role and create a different kind of relationship with her. Moreover, better informed and more independent, she wants to work with a salesperson who will assist her in making decisions. The buyer has more choices and therefore can be more selective about where she takes her business. She does not have to put up with salespeople or organizations that do not cater to her needs.

Today's buyer is more value-conscious. In addition to the specific benefits of the product or service, she is looking for value-added services from the relationship. And in some types of buying, other people inside the organization are involved with her in the decision-making process, thereby making it more complex. Open, honest communication from a trusted salesperson makes her more effective internally.

A salesperson today wants changes also. He is unhappy with the pressure and the grind of constantly searching for new business. He prefers to work in long-term relationships with customers so he can have a greater impact on the results for his clients. Also, a salesperson wants to make a difference for his customers; therefore, he wants to have an ongoing relationship so that he can be sure his customer receives the quality of service he promised. Further, a salesperson wants more autonomy and authority in dealing with his customers.

Finally, salespeople want to be treated fairly, with respect and recognition for the job they are doing. Most believe in their product or service and know they could do great things if given the opportunity. The bottom line is that salespeople today want their job to be a source of greater pride and satisfaction.

The traditional approach to the seller-buyer relationship does not satisfy the needs of the marketplace, of buyers, or of salespeople themselves. Other factors, such as the way salespeople are managed, the way they are trained, and the way they are motivated, perpetuate the problem. The entire sales system is broken.

What's needed is a transformation of the profession. This transformation must be fundamental and pervasive and impact the entire system. Not only must there be a major shift in the type of relationship a salesperson builds with her buyers, but also in the relationships she has with her manager and other departments involved in the selling-buying process. Furthermore, the quality and type of training that she receives must change to match the skills needed in her new role. And finally, the very organizational culture she works in must alter to support the transformation. Let's examine what's actually happening today in those areas.

RELATIONSHIPS BETWEEN SELLERS AND BUYERS

In an article about our Synergistic Selling training program, writer John Stoler put it this way (notice how he uses masculine pronouns to reinforce the traditional thinking about selling):

> The image of the salesperson has been tarnished and stereotyped since the snake sold Eve a bite of the apple and Eve, in turn, convinced Adam that munching on the forbidden fruit was a good idea for him, too. For his success, the snake was cursed by the Lord and condemned to a life on his belly with dust as his nourishment. How unfair. In any other organization, the snake would receive a commission, a bonus, and the promise of a vice-presidency if he kept up the good work. And Eve would have been hired on the spot, a born "natural."
>
> And the image lingers. Salesman—an oily snake in the grass, slithering deviously around, plotting and scheming to sell something unwanted, or more than is needed, to an unsuspecting mark. He comes on strong, aggressive, superior, and overwhelming.

He has something he "knows" is needed and a canned response to every doubt and obstacle thrown in his path. His job is to lead the prospect through a labyrinth of corridors, eliciting a positive response at every turn, until he walks away with a signed order. The customer is his opponent, someone to be overcome and beaten.

Of course, many salespeople will say they don't work that way, but that is not the point. What we want to emphasize is that this is the context in which we sell. The selling-buying process generally occurs with the perception that someone is going to win and someone is going to lose. This is the reason it is so difficult to develop a high degree of trust in a seller-buyer relationship. Just stand in a retail store and watch the dynamics. A salesperson approaches a buyer and says, "May I help you?" and most shoppers respond, "No thanks, I'm just browsing," as they continue looking.

Sales has been about closing the sale. Buyers are very aware that this means that it's the seller's job to consummate the deal through whatever means possible. They know that salespeople have been trained to do just that and that, in many cases, the salesperson's compensation is based on their ability to succeed in that purpose.

There is also an unwritten assumption that a good salesperson should be able to overcome any obstacle, including a mismatch between his product and the needs of the buyer. In our seminars, it is amazing how many salespeople think that they should close every sale and that they've done something wrong if they don't. They live in the belief that selling is like playing a chess game with the buyer. At the conclusion, there is a winner and a loser. Someone will get their needs met and someone won't. If your strategies and tactics are sound, you'll win. Obviously, this attitude sets salespeople up for a great deal of frustration.

This win-lose approach can be very costly. John, a sales manager for a major U.S. airline, provided this example. His airline skillfully negotiated an agreement with a major corporation in one of their key markets. The client agreed to produce a certain volume of business at a certain price. It was a comprehensive agreement that both parties put a lot of work into, and each felt that they had a strong relationship with the other.

At the conclusion of the first year of the contract, senior management at the airline took a tough stance in negotiating a new agreement. Their market share had increased, and they felt confident in taking this position. In looking back at it, John used the analogy of a marriage and said it was as if his company had said to the other one, "I shouldn't have married you, and I want a divorce." And this divorce was very painful. The client got very upset, tempers flared, accusations were thrown back and forth, and by the time management realized the impact of their position, it was too late. They lost a $4 million annual account to a competitor. The chess game was over. They had lost.

In this case, the client got back at the airline by taking its business elsewhere. Here's an example of how salespeople can get back at clients. Charles is a sales manager in the agriculture products division of a major U.S. corporation. He remembers Bob, the vice president of an agricultural cooperative who thought it was his job to beat down all salespeople. He simply made life for salespeople miserable. For a while Charles succumbed to the pressure and made several short-term price concessions to the cooperative just to get Bob off his back. But then he'd had enough, and he discovered ways he could get back at Bob. First of all, whenever he had the power to make the decision, he said no to any special requests from the cooperative. Furthermore, Charles made a preferred cost deal with Bob's competitor, who also supplied products to the farmers. That gave Bob's competitor a price advantage in the marketplace. And finally, Charles delayed the delivery of new products to Bob's cooperative to again impact his position with the farmers. It had become a serious game of one-upmanship.

The power struggle between buyers and sellers in the traditional approach to selling produces winners and losers.

Winning and losing in a relationship is determined by whether or not your needs are met. In the traditional win-lose type of selling, one person satisfies her needs at the expense of the other person. Here is an exercise to illustrate the consequences of this win-lose approach:

> First, think back to a time in your life when you lost and the other person won. The most obvious examples are conflicts with other people when they used their authority and forced a solution to the conflict on you. Perhaps your parents grounded you or took the car away for coming in late, or a teacher punished you in front of the class, or a customer threatened to cancel their business unless you gave in on a certain issue.
>
> Then think about what you did in response to their use of power over you. Identify the feelings you were experiencing about the situation and the other person. And, finally, think about the effects that event had on the relationship.

In situations like these, the person being dominated resorts to defense mechanisms to cope with the power. Some people resist or rebel openly; others drop out; others withdraw and become depressed. These alternatives could also be called *fight, flight,* or *submit.*

FIGHT

Naturally, one of your alternatives is to fight back, or find some way to get back at the other person. You may decide to go over the other person's head and talk to their boss, or get back at a customer by not passing along a special price consideration. In one of our seminars, a participant confessed to faking the information on a new field research report that he had been ordered to complete, just to get it done. That was his way of fighting back. There are many subtle and manipulative ways that people "fight back."

FLIGHT

With this option, you simply choose to abandon the relationship, whether mentally or physically. In the extreme, you quit the company or completely avoid the other person. In one of our client organizations, we discovered that one department was faxing information to another department three offices away simply as a way of ignoring them. In another situation, we uncovered almost a million dollars in outstanding receivables due to one department's avoiding another and not resolving some internal problems on the invoices, thus holding up the billing. Most salespeople can relate to putting off a difficult phone call to an intimidating customer that is on their to-do list Monday morning. You know the situation: Monday gets very busy, and Tuesday you're swamped after sales meeting. Wednesday and Thursday you're out on calls, and Friday you have some calls to return immediately. So the difficult call gets carried over to next Monday's to-do list.

Perhaps the saddest example of flight is when the individual leaves the relationship mentally but not physically. Organizations are full of "dead" people walking the hallways and filling office space. You see these people frequently— they've given up, resigned themselves to the status quo. And, in a "flight" mode, buyers just sit there and listen to your presentation with no intention of buying.

SUBMIT

In this option, you give in. Perhaps you feel that you don't have a choice, or you don't want to upset the other person. Whatever the reason, you acquiesce and sabotage your own needs. This alternative is dangerous for three reasons. First, you damage your own self-esteem when your needs aren't met. Second, you keep score, intending at some time in the future to get back at the other person. Third, many people keep their feelings bottled up inside. When this occurs, they may blow up at others for no apparent reason, or they may develop stress-related illnesses, or even escape with food, drugs, or alcohol.

These are the typical reactions to "control" in the traditional win-lose model. Many individuals see no other options, and they then become very adept at denying their feelings and rationalizing their behavior. Their motto is "That's just the way it is!"

The key word that usually comes up in our seminars to describe people's feelings about losing is *resentment*. Losers resent winners, and someone generally loses in the traditional approach to selling. The resulting resentment manifests itself in many ways. In even the simplest seller-buyer interaction, a buyer's resentment shows thoughts like these: "If I don't believe I'll get my needs met, I will shut the door and not let you in; or if you are real persistent, or nice, I will politely listen to your presentation and then say, 'I'll think about it.' "

Buyers who don't satisfy their needs with sellers also do such things as form alliances to enhance their buying power, take their business elsewhere without complaining, hide out behind their voice mail, or don't return phone calls. Others demand special considerations or drag out decisions because they don't have enough information to feel comfortable about making a decision. Still others supply you with very little information about their needs or tell you just to provide the necessary information and they will make the decision.

On the flip side, when salespeople don't get their needs met, the resentment also surfaces in many ways. Salespeople increase the pressure another notch, find ways to go around the buyer when possible, or don't quote the best prices on future agreements. Or they don't return phone calls or don't share all pertinent information. Others turn their resentment inward and subordinate themselves to buyers, damaging their self-confidence and becoming less assertive. And many turn their resentment in other directions and blame outside factors for their results: the economy; the pricing structure; or other departments, such as manufacturing or customer support.

Sounds pretty familiar, doesn't it? Remember, *losers resent winners*. Both buyers and sellers develop their own ways of avoiding domination, all of which block the flow of communication and perpetuate the adversarial nature of the relationship. Examine the problems you have with buyers right now, and you'll trace them back to a win-lose interaction.

The traditional model of relating to buyers is simply ineffective and obsolete.

RELATIONSHIPS WITH SALES MANAGERS

Participants in our Synergistic Selling training course tell some frightening stories about their sales managers. They share examples of sales managers who use tricks, gimmicks, manipulation, fear, and even coercive power to motivate their salespeople.

LaVonne, a salesperson with an apparel manufacturing company, told the following story about the problem she was having with her new manager. The threats and other techniques he employed to motivate her to improve her performance were having the opposite effect. She felt pressured and not supported. As a result, she began to doubt her abilities and question everything she was doing. Her production dropped, which prompted even more pressure. At the time of our course, she was in a real slump. The final blow had occurred earlier in the month when her sales manager insisted she call in after every sales call and leave a message on his voice mail. When she objected, he replied, "I'm your boss and don't forget it." LaVonne was at a loss about what to do. She'd been with the company for over seven years and had a good track record, but she was ready to give up and resign.

Howard, a business development manager for a major automotive financing company, told how his boss kept changing his scheduled sales appointments at the last minute. Whenever the operations people got behind in responding to dealer financing applications (a frequent problem), Howard's manager would pull him in to help out because he had a strong background in that department. This meant constantly canceling and rescheduling sales appointments. His frustration was compounded by the fact that he thought the department could be managed more effectively and the problem solved in other ways. Furthermore, he resented being yanked about at someone else's whim. But when he complained, Howard was told that there was no other option and that he should just be a good soldier and follow orders. Howard was quite frustrated with this situation as he knew he was being evaluated on his sales performance.

After hearing hundreds of examples like these, we have developed a radical belief: if an organization wants to increase its sales performance, it should get rid of most sales managers, or train them in a new set of interpersonal and leadership skills. It's logical. If you remove the obstacles to the sales process, sales will improve. Too many sales managers today are controlling, autocratic, dictatorial, and demotivating. It's the same thing that prompted Tom Peters and Robert Waterman, Jr., to write their book *In Search of Excellence:* "Talented teachers and gifted students in sales management . . . are still as scarce (and refreshing) as rain in the desert."

The prevalent model of sales management practiced today is one of planning, controlling, justifying, manipulating, and motivating by fear. This results in high turnover in the vital sales positions where buyers want to build ongoing relationships with knowledgeable, experienced people and costly periods of lower productivity for the new salespeople. Additionally, knowing the high turnover in these positions, many organizations don't invest in training their salespeople, yielding a less-than-effective sales effort. This management style also produces morale problems, and then expensive annual sales meetings and incentive programs are designed to motivate the unmotivated sales team. Management teams spend more time justifying the slow sales than understanding and correcting the core issues. The bottom line—lower sales levels than the organization is capable of producing.

Then upper management gets frustrated and applies more threats, more incentives, and more pressure. These tools backfire again, producing a drop in morale, and the cycle begins again. Obviously, those making these decisions haven't learned Rita Mae Brown's definition of insanity: "Doing the same thing over and over again and expecting different results."

The authoritative management style that permeates most sales organizations is a costly practice in today's competitive and challenging marketplace. Or, to put it another way, *it simply doesn't work.* Following is a list of the consequences of this win-lose management style (these items should, by now, be familiar to all managers):

A REDUCTION IN UPWARD COMMUNICATION

One of the most damaging effects on organizational effectiveness is the noticeable reduction in communication from the salespeople who have direct contact with customers to the people who can do something about any problems. When communication is passed "up the ladder," it is carefully screened so as to not upset the boss. This severely hampers an organization's ability to react to customer needs and problems.

DEVELOPMENT OF A "YES-MAN" CULTURE

In an authoritative sales management culture, salespeople find it easier to agree with the boss rather than confront difficult issues. This "shoot the messenger" attitude stifles the flow of accurate information essential for effective problem-solving, and the obstacles to sales effectiveness remain untouched.

DESTRUCTIVE COMPETITIVENESS AND RIVALRY

The basic tenet here is simple: "If I can make others look bad, I may look better by comparison; if I can blame others, I may be able to avoid punishment." Competition and rivalry among members of the sales team are the antithesis of the cooperation and team play needed in an effective sales organization today.

SUBMISSION AND CONFORMITY

Some salespeople choose obedience and compliance, passively bowing down to the authoritative sales manager. They believe they will get rewarded by doing exactly what they are told and nothing more. The problem here is that these people are usually weak in initiative and low in commitment and creativity—not the kind of salespeople you want in the field today.

REBELLION AND DEFIANCE

The opposite of submission and conformity is rebellion and defiance, stances taken by salespeople who either resist anything the sales manager wants to do or turn around and do the opposite. Resistance by rebellious group members frustrates and irritates others who want to move ahead and solve problems. Defiant salespeople slow down the group because their arguments and disagreements must be dealt with. Rebellion and defiance are defenses against being dominated or controlled.

WITHDRAWING AND ESCAPE

Some salespeople cope with an authoritative management style by finding ways to remove themselves from the relationship—either physically or psychologically. They may avoid sales managers, avoid speaking up in sales meetings, or even leave the company.

The relationship between salespeople and sales managers must improve. The existing relationship undermines the sales organization's performance in the marketplace. Once again, the present system isn't working effectively.

RELATIONSHIPS WITH OTHERS INVOLVED IN
THE SELLING-BUYING PROCESS

Gone are the simple days of salespeople being issued a product and told to go sell it. From selling real estate to selling complex computer systems, from selling manufactured products to selling intangible services, we work in a very complex business environment. In real estate, in addition to their buyer, agents work with the seller, lending institutions, title or escrow companies, and, perhaps, outside contractors. The sale can fall apart if anything goes wrong anywhere in the process. Likewise, a salesperson in the corporate arena has other departments within the organization and maybe even some outside contacts that are all instrumental in the selling and servicing process. The point is, the relationship between the seller and the buyer is not the only relationship essential to successful selling today.

To make a sale and to maintain the seller-buyer relationship, a complex network of interdependent individuals must be managed, and a salesperson must coordinate the different agendas of this team of individuals. Moreover, the salesperson has to communicate customer needs back to the organization for appropriate product-service design and marketing. In addition, a salesperson may have to make commitments for the other team members to implement. She also has to coordinate problem solving among customers and other departments when something breaks down in the process.

Thus salespeople act as a critical middle person between customers and the company. In today's complex organizations, this role can become very frustrating, as the following story demonstrates.

Scott is a major account representative for a large uniform manufacturer with an annual sales volume of about $180 million. He recently spent a lot of time and effort tying down a contract to supply uniforms for an automotive company's dealerships. This was a major account for Scott and his company as the total contract was worth about $2 million in sales. He and the client developed a forecast based on past uniform usage at the dealerships and sent it to the home office to begin production.

Tom is the customer-service manager responsible for implementing Scott's contract. His job is to coordinate the work between production and the inventory control department. Under pressure to minimize inventory levels during a tight cash-flow period, he and the inventory control department cut back the forecast and, therefore, production of the uniforms. As a result, the company ran out of stock in the first thirty days of the new program. The dealers couldn't get the uniforms the company had been promoting, and they were complaining. Scott's client was furious.

The client called and yelled at Scott, and he turned around and called Tom to find out what had gone wrong. When he found out the forecast had been arbitrarily cut back, he got upset and called Tom's boss, who said he'd look into it. The client, in the meantime, wrote a letter to Scott and to the president of the company. The president jumped in, ordered an increase in production, and seemed to take care of the problem. However, the customer was bitter; he felt Scott had let him down. Scott lost the trusted relationship with the client that he had spent months building.

The client then requested a plan of action (a service agreement) on how the organization would avoid this situation in the future. Tom declined to write the plan as he considered it a "political football," so Scott wrote the plan, reviewed it with his client, and sent it to Tom and Tom's boss for approval. After not hearing anything for more than thirty days, he started making phone calls and finally, to his surprise, received a totally new plan that Tom had written. This new plan was unacceptable to the client, as it included some new financial guarantees that had not been discussed. Scott then went to his boss, who went to Tom's boss and the vice president of marketing.

After six months of departmental bickering, blame-filled meetings in the home office, writing and rewriting the service agreement, and finally getting everyone's approval, Scott walked into the client's office with the new plan. In addition to an upset client who was now on his back about everything that went wrong, Scott had lost his credibility and his friendship with the client. Furthermore, he had spent a great deal of frustrating time documenting his actions and trying to get the problem resolved with the home office. He remembers going home at night and wanting to hit his head against the wall as he wondered if it was all worth it.

Then, to top it all off, his "attitude" was pointed out on his next evaluation. Did the hoopla and glamour of the national sales meeting enhance Scott's motivation? No way. He and the other salespeople experiencing similar frustrations used the opportunity to commiserate with each other.

Not all problems are that complex, but they can be just as frustrating for salespeople. Eric, a salesperson for a commercial printing company, complains about the delays in getting project bids from the estimating department for his customers. It's a constant hassle for him just to bring in new business. Patrick, an independent insurance agent, talks about his problems in getting new policies approved through the underwriting department. He even avoids one particular underwriter because of the tension in the relationship, which slows down the whole process. And Teri, a real estate agent, tells of the time a lending institution demanded more documentation three days before the closing of a sale, killing the sale and destroying the moving schedule of three families.

When breakdowns occur, a conflict develops, and in the traditional win-lose relationship model, resentment surfaces in many ways. Interdepartmental communication gets stifled, and as a result, core issues are seldom addressed. Departments and/or individuals blame each other, thereby blocking effective problem solving. The culture is therefore one of crisis management. A great deal of time and money are wasted.

Individuals and departments build "empires" to protect themselves. Others have difficulty approaching them. The open flow of vital communications is prevented. Some individuals go around the obstacle, and the system is short-circuited, yielding no accountability. Still others hide out behind "company policy" and limit the flexibility needed to meet changing customer needs.

"We" and "they" feelings are generated between the home office and the field sales personnel, and the customers get caught in the middle. This is why so many salespeople in our courses tell us they feel as if they're working against the people in the home office to bring in customers and then to properly service them.

Another example reinforces these points. The Synergistic Selling program was recently delivered to a hundred-person field sales force of a $200 million manufacturing company. As the company grew, they created the job of sales administration manager (SAM). This position was designed to handle the communications among the field sales personnel and marketing, manufacturing, product development, and other departments in the home office. However, when the salespeople didn't get the answers they wanted from the SAMs or didn't get them when they wanted them, their "fight, flight, or submit" reactions emerged in full force. The internal support people, the SAMs, were caught in the middle, and each side began blaming the other when the system broke down. At the time of the sales training, it became obvious that the system was in shambles.

Some salespeople, especially the experienced individuals who were used to the old system, went around their SAM to operational departments to get answers, thus sabotaging any chance for the SAM to be effective.

Many SAMs resented certain salespeople and followed up on their work last, if at all. Others built strong relationships with internal departments and then teamed up against the salespeople when company policy wasn't followed.

Individuals in manufacturing and other operational departments resented it when the SAM or field salesperson used "customer service" as a club to get them to do something. These people shut themselves off from both the SAMs and the salespeople.

The system didn't work: the culture was one of finger-pointing and politics. Everyone worked while looking over their shoulder to protect their backside. It's no wonder the company's market share had deteriorated dramatically in recent years.

These problems run rampant in organizations, and most people take them for granted. They shrug and say, "That's just the way it is around here." They are resigned to working in the existing system and simply making the best of it. The system is broken. But the relationships between salespeople and others who impact the selling-buying process are too critical to continue in their present manner.

SALES TRAINING

Selling today must be seen as a profession that requires both knowledge and skills. It's a disgrace how many organizations don't provide any training at all for their salespeople. Without training, the very lifeblood of an organization isn't being properly prepared to perform the vital job of selling.

Organizations that don't provide formal training or those that turn down requests from salespeople who want to be reimbursed for a five-hundred-dollar seminar, are sending a loud message: YOU ARE NOT IMPORTANT! It is often a vicious cycle—managers say they can't afford to send people for training to improve their ability to bring in more business, yet they know that untrained people are not effective at bringing in business. So business doesn't get better, and then it follows that they can't provide training for their people. Remember: *If you always do what you've always done, you'll always get what you've always gotten.*

Carolyn recalls her first sales job in the hotel business. She reported to work, was given a tour of the hotel, and then was told to report to housekeeping. She spent the next month learning the operational departments: housekeeping, reservations, front desk, kitchen, restaurants, catering, and convention services. At the conclusion of her "training," she reported to the sales department and was handed a stack of files and spent some time with the secretary learning the procedures.

After a sincere "good luck" comment from her sales manager, she started her sales career.

Reflecting back, she remembers how unsure and easily intimidated she was. Oh, sure she could make a bed, reserve a room, or serve a meal. But she was lost sitting across the desk from a client who could bring in tens of thousands of dollars in revenue for her hotel.

Many organizations do just that. They teach salespeople the operational aspects of the business and then send them out into the competitive marketplace to bring in some business.

Untrained salespeople are left on their own to figure out how to make sales. Most salespeople are uncomfortable in their selling role and don't like the stereotype of salespeople. So, rather than become a "typical pushy salesperson," many go to the other extreme and are far too passive. This is one of the reasons research studies show that a majority of sales calls end with the salesperson's never asking the buyer for their business. Sending salespeople out to do their job without training is like asking them to jump out of a plane without a parachute. In both cases, there is no doubt about the result.

Without taking a proactive role and training its salespeople, an organization is putting its fate into the hands of external circumstances. That is why the economy, the competition, and other factors yank and pull on the organization's results.

In those organizations where formal sales training is provided, it is usually product-oriented—product training and more product training. Granted, salespeople must have a working knowledge of their products, but a lot of the training may not be essential. In fact, if salespeople openly admit that they don't know the answer to a technical question posed by the buyer, they can always call for technical support. That, in itself, may enhance their credibility. Typically, the more a salesperson depends upon product knowledge, the stronger the desire to share that wisdom and the less likely it is that they'll listen to their customer and find out her actual needs. When you are entrenched in the traditional model of selling, product knowledge seems essential to produce slick presentations, to overcome all objections, and to maintain complete control of the sales call.

Even when "sales technique" training is provided, it is often "psychobabble"—techniques to psychoanalyze the buyer and dominate him. Paul laughs as he talks about the training he received as a new recruit for a stock brokerage firm: two weeks in New York City on how to control the buyer's thinking to get him to buy. And this was from a company that promoted the fact that they listened to their customers.

Traditional training teaches a series of sales-controlled steps thought necessary to close a sale. When you sit back and look at it carefully, what salespeople are taught is really incredible. From the bookshelves overflowing with "how-to" books to the hundreds of sales audiocassette training tapes, and including in-house company-developed training programs, as well as outside seminars and speakers, the message is always the same: tips, tactics, techniques, and strategies to control the steps of the sales process—to win the "chess game."

Several years ago *Training* magazine ran an article on the current state of sales training. In this article, David Merges, a sales trainer for the Miller Brewing Company, chuckles at the things salespeople are expected to learn:

> Things like (take a deep breath) prospecting, qualifying, probing, listening, presenting, questioning, supporting, closing, proving, explaining, refocusing, building, overcoming objections, planning, problem-solving, and managing their time. They also have to learn to ask all sorts of questions, such as open, closed, discovery, leading, standard tie-down, inverted tie-down, internal tie-down, tag-on tie-down, clarifying and opinion.
>
> Wait there's more. Salespeople have to learn how to close, of course, and that's no simple matter either. There's the summary close, the alternative close, the impending event, the test, the trail, the erroneous conclusion, the porcupine test, the crash and burn, the moving to the major, the basic, the "let me

make a note of that," the sharp-angle, the Ben Franklin, the similar situation, the Dear Old Mom, the I'll think it over, and the no close at all.

Salespeople are inundated with techniques thought to control the sales process, to "read" the buyer, to "probe" for the information that they need to make the presentation, to "overcome objections," and to "close" the sale. Because the model is built on an adversarial competition between the buyer and seller, in order to be successful, the seller must be skilled at maintaining the upper hand without the buyer's knowing it.

There are countless examples showing how traditional sales training emphasizes and reinforces the traditional adversarial nature of the seller-buyer relationship. The manipulative techniques and the language of control to which salespeople are constantly exposed keep them mired in the traditional model of selling and limit their success in today's marketplace.

THE ORGANIZATIONAL CULTURE

Many graduates of our Synergistic Selling program leave with enthusiasm and commitment to the new model of selling. Once they are back within a culture not designed to support their change, they find themselves very frustrated. As a result of this feedback, we have done a lot of work with our clients in addressing the organizational issues that impact the effectiveness of the salespeople. What we discovered is really no surprise: *today's organizational cultures and the systems designed within that culture are primitive and ineffective when held up against the challenges and demands of the business environment.* The cultures reinforce and perpetuate the traditional model of selling that is self-defeating in the marketplace.

It's time the organization lived up to its responsibility to provide a stimulating and supportive environment in which committed individuals can grow. The organization can consciously plan to make the necessary changes, or it can be forced into it by the demands of the business environment.

In actuality, not much has changed between the management culture found in most organizations today and the plantation system of the Old South. Since the time of the plantation system, great technological changes have taken place in our society, yet our human relations skills are as primitive as ever.

In her book *Beyond Power*, Marilyn French puts it this way: "To keep a slave in a ditch, one must stay there oneself, or appoint an overseer to guarantee the slave's obedience. But then it is necessary to appoint a supervisor who will make sure that the slave and the overseer do not collude; then a governor who will make sure all three do not collude . . . and so on."

True, the physical working conditions in today's organizations are better than those on the plantation, and the management techniques more subtle, yet the whip is still there. You'll still hear the term "slave driver" used when referring to supervisors seemingly indifferent to the needs of their employees. The use of reward and punishment to get people to do their job is still standard operating procedure. In many organizations, even the modern concept of "empowerment" is another form of manipulation to get employees to do what management want them to do.

Most sales organizations—like plantations—create annual objectives and then tell each salesperson (slave) the results expected from them in order for the annual plan (harvest goals) to be achieved. Salespeople must perform, or wages, benefits, and other privileges will be taken away. Forms of discipline such as written notices become the order of the day. Top salespeople are paraded before their peers as role models of hard workers. Managers (overseers) are asked for greater production while the CEOs (plantation owners) stride benevolently through the offices espousing the benefits of working for the company (plantation).

The waste of human talent inside today's organizations is appalling. There is a tremendous drain of human resources and capabilities. Some people get fed up and leave, while others decide to stay physically but have checked out mentally. Many do just what's needed to get by, and still others simply mark the days until the weekend, their vacation, or their retirement. In many organizations, this situation is simply accepted as "That's just the way it is, and it won't ever change" or "That's just the nature of human beings; you can't depend on anyone to do a good job anymore." In others, key managers are fired, laid off, or moved aside because they can't "motivate the team." In still other organizations, new training programs are implemented, new incentive plans announced, and "motivational" sales meetings are held. All are designed to "fix the problem," assuming the people are the problem. That is, the object of these programs is to get salespeople enthusiastic about their job and to improve their performance. In most organizations, these attempts to "fix the people" are seen as subtle "whips" to manipulate behavior and, therefore, don't work. If anything, these traditional remedies are detrimental, since they simply perpetuate the existing culture. And the waste continues.

Today's modern, technologically advanced, complex organizations are operating with a structure probably developed in the very primitive beginnings of man. Yet this structure is taken for granted, and for most, there is no other way. It is so ingrained in us, that few people can think of options. It limits organizational effectiveness.

The traditional hierarchy is visually reproduced on the organization chart. The boxes, the lines, the dotted lines, and the multiple layers of management found on the typical organization chart do make it easy to identify who's who, to see some semblance of a line of authority, and to recognize the path of a nice communication flow. But anyone who has worked in a large organization knows that in actuality the organization chart used to show hierarchy has major defects.

First of all, it reflects only "positional power." It does not identify those individuals you go to to get things done—the people who can get through the maze of the system and make things really happen. In other words, it depicts those individuals who have played the game effectively, not to be confused with those who have been effective. This is not meant as a criticism of these individuals. They are merely products of the existing culture. They have successfully played by the rules of the accepted game. It's the game and its rules that are wrong, not the individuals. However, even though it is difficult for these people to let go of the rules for success that have made them successful, they must recognize that the game is changing. Perhaps the biggest danger to today's organization is the complacency with which these individuals hold on to the existing game simply because they cannot see other possibilities.

The organization chart uses boxes to identify positions, but they actually reflect roadblocks to go around to get things done. It does not accurately represent the communication channels that have been developed out of necessity to move around the obstacles. Additionally, it shows the empires created by departmental function, but not the conflicts inherent in the design.

Multiple layers of management are identified, but not the limited communication flow between those layers. Important information essential for effective decisions at the "top" of the hierarchy usually gets filtered through the lower levels of management, where it's massaged so that it will be more acceptable to those hearing it. Communication is distorted by individuals desiring to look good and to maneuver for power. The information flow is blocked by fear and trust issues inherent in the design, and its content is watered down so as not to exacerbate the unresolved conflicts not reflected on the organization chart.

In addition, the chart does not reflect the inordinate amount of time required to address customer-service and product-quality issues. These issues, so fundamental to the sales process, affect customer-contact employees, who are usually on the bottom of the chart.

The traditional hierarchy is confining, inadequate, and ineffective for dealing with the needs of today's business environment.

Another area of the organization's culture that perpetuates the problem is the quota system. The underlying message behind "quota" is "These are the results you are expected to produce; do anything you can to achieve these numbers, except drop the price."

In the organizations that operate with a strong monthly quota system, the customers simply become numbers. They are the obstacles on the path toward achieving one's quotas. Since many salespeople have a specific market area and regularly call on the same customers, these customers become the same obstacles monthly, quarterly, or annually. The priority becomes producing numbers rather than building a strong base of loyal customers.

Here's an example from the automotive industry involving the salespeople in the parts division who call on the same automobile dealerships every month.

The last week of the month, the orders would come down from upstairs: "We are short our quota—get out there and move parts!" The salespeople would then call the dealerships and beg, call in favors, or do anything else necessary to move more product. Little wonder that the dealers weren't happy to see them on the next visit. They had too much inventory and were always complaining about something. It's no surprise that the sales-training classes in this company were predominantly focused on handling customer problems and complaints.

Similar situations occur in other companies. Quotas are established by upper management, who then develop reward systems to try to see that the quotas are met. The whole system makes the problem worse. In an effort to increase sales, a structure is developed that is actually detrimental to the primary objective: increasing revenue.

The relationship between buyers and sellers is fragile to begin with, and it becomes even more complicated when systems are put in place which create more tension and resistance. The results are seldom what is expected. The Sears organization noticed this in June 1992, when two states, California and New Jersey, accused it of fraudulent activities in selling unnecessary auto repairs to their customers. Within a week, Sears came out with an announcement that out of their commitment to their customers and to avoid any additional problems, they were changing the incentive-compensation and goal-setting systems for their automotive repair people. Evidently Sears saw that it had created an environment in which customers could be abused. So the company changed to a system that rewarded customer satisfaction.

The quota system needs dramatic overhaul. In addition to the pressure it puts on the seller-buyer relationship, it doesn't work. First, we know that salespeople are less motivated to achieve goals forced on them by upper management; and, second, reward systems fail when they are seen as coercive and manipulative. If salespeople are not allowed to participate in setting their goals and if quotas don't seem attainable, no incentives will change their behavior.

The quota system used by so many organizations today is detrimental to the success it was designed to create. Once again, a change is needed to maximize the effectiveness of salespeople in today's marketplace.

BUSINESS AS USUAL CAN NO LONGER BE TOLERATED

As we've said throughout this chapter, today's marketplace demands a new relationship model between sellers and buyers, between salespeople and their sales managers, and between salespeople and the others who impact the selling process. Furthermore, the way salespeople are trained and the culture they work in must change to support the new model.

Not only is the system in need of repair, but the typical solutions or attempts to repair it don't work either. The standard methods of fixing the problems are working harder, developing stronger rewards and punishments, spending time in meetings discussing the problem, blaming outside events or the economy, or even changing the people. None of these methods seems to work, which just adds to the frustration of everyone involved in selling today. The traditional system of selling is like a car that has seen its days of glory. It's too old to repair and it's not economically feasible to pour any more money into it. It's time to buy a new one.

The pressure for performance is intense. To compete, or even survive, individuals and organizations must look for new solutions to the challenges of selling. A little more, a little better, a little different, won't suffice. Only a significant shift in our thinking will produce results—a paradigm shift for the profession of sales.

Chapter Summary

1. To keep pace with the needs of an ever-changing business environment, success in selling today requires a radical departure from traditional thinking.
2. Several factors are driving this change:
   - the technological complexity of the marketplace;
   - a stronger need for building and maintaining long-term relationships with customers due to increased competition and the cost of bringing in new business compared to the lower cost of keeping existing customers happy;
   - the quality movement demands closer partnership between buyers and sellers;
   - both sellers and buyers want a change in the relationship.
3. This transformation must address five fundamental areas:
   - the relationship between buyers and sellers;
   - the relationship between salespeople and their sales managers;
   - the relationship between salespeople and others involved in the selling process;
   - the sales training provided salespeople;
   - the organizational culture in which salespeople work.

4. The traditional "close the sale" mentality is obsolete in today's marketplace.
5. The prevalent model of sales management practiced is demotivating and has severe consequences to overall sales effectiveness.
6. As sales becomes more complex, salespeople must manage an interdependent network of individuals that impact the selling process.
7. The training that salespeople receive today is insufficient to prepare them for the challenges of the marketplace.
8. The culture in sales organizations today perpetuates the traditional thinking about sales and limits sales effectiveness.
9. What's needed is a transformation, a paradigm shift, in the profession of selling.

CHAPTER TWO

THE PARADIGM

SHIFT IN SALES

*The real act of discovery consists not in finding new lands,
but in seeing with new eyes.*

—*MARCEL PROUST*

The word *paradigm* comes from the Greek root, *paradeigma*,
which means "model or pattern." A paradigm is a system of
thinking that forms the basis for how we look at and experience life. Therefore, paradigms determine how we perceive
our world. They form the basis for our "reality."

In his book *Discovering the Future: The Business of Paradigms*, Joel Barker offers this current definition of a paradigm: "A paradigm is a set of rules and regulations that: (1)
defines boundaries and (2) tells you what to do to be successful within those boundaries." In other words, a paradigm is a
set of beliefs that form very specific boundaries as to what is

acceptable and what is not. Considering that a paradigm is a multifaceted abstraction, let's examine the four primary principles, or facets, of paradigms to add some clarity.

A paradigm is a pattern of thinking that determines how we look at life. It actually filters our experience to match our beliefs. Perhaps this analogy will help you to understand the power of paradigms. In photography, you may be aware that you can put filters over the camera lens to change what the camera records on film. There are filters to make the sky darker and more dramatic, to soften the focus for portraits, to give a dramatic starry effect to lights, and many others. When a filter is on the camera lens, the camera sees a new "reality." And you can change the "reality" that the camera sees by changing the filter.

Paradigms work the same way. They filter our experience of life to form a "reality" that matches our beliefs. Notice in the drawing below the paradigm effect.

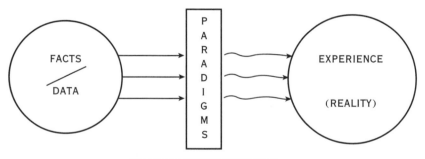

FILTERS / INTERPRETATIONS

Our paradigms act as filters interpreting what happens in life (the facts) to form our experience (our reality). For example, if you believe that you can't trust your boss and she comes to you and says, "Great job on the Miller account. I think you really handled it well," what you'll probably think is, "I wonder what she wants" or "She's just a phony." We discount any evidence that contradicts our operating paradigms.

Paradigms are invisible and exist below our level of consciousness. Therefore, they are rarely recognized, examined, or even understood. They are the invisible forces that form the boundaries of our lives, like the invisible glass of the aquarium that forms the boundaries of the fish's world. Most people rarely examine the paradigms influencing their lives and, therefore, live in the restricted environment of the fishbowl. They think and behave within consistent patterns determined by their prevalent paradigms.

Paradigms define, limit, and influence our behavior. They shape what we think and what we don't think, what we say and what we don't say. Our paradigms influence our life as the railroad track influences the behavior of a train. Most people think they control their lives, but that control is just as limited as the control an engineer has over a train. In actuality, the only influence the engineer has is over the speed. He can make the train slow down or speed up. Just as the railroad tracks determine the direction of the train, so too do our paradigms shape the direction of our lives.

Furthermore, if your paradigms remain the same, your future is very predictable. Like the train on the railroad track always following the same route to the same destination, without a change in your paradigms, your future will simply be an extension of your past. To ignore the power of paradigms to shape what is possible is to severely limit your ability to make changes in your life.

Because paradigms define our behavior, they provide a set of rules for us to follow to be successful within that paradigm. For example, the game of baseball has very specific rules and regulations, and players know what has to be done to be successful within the boundaries of those rules. If the pitcher throws four balls outside the strike zone, the batter gets to walk to first base, or if he throws three balls inside the strike zone, the batter is out. After three outs, the other team gets its chance to score runs, and so on. These rules limit players' behavior to that which is acceptable according to the rules. In other words, the batter cannot hit the ball to the outfield and run directly to third base without paying the consequences—being called out.

Even though they are not written down, our paradigms establish rules that are just as powerful as the rules of baseball. They are unseen and many times unspoken, but they are just the same. In a business context, for example, everyone could describe the IBM look: the dark suit, white shirt, and wingtip shoes for men and an equally conservative look for women. The dress code that influenced what IBM employees wore for many years is not written down, yet, until recently, no one within the company would dare dress differently. In the last few years, that has changed, reflecting the changing beliefs at IBM. Our paradigms work the same.

Paradigms shape what is possible and what is achievable. Because they form the boundaries of our lives, they effectively limit possibilities that we perceive as being outside those boundaries.

Likewise, what is defined as impossible today is impossible only from the perception of your present paradigms. For example, prior to 1492, it was impossible to travel around the world. The prevailing thinking, the paradigm, of the time was that the earth was flat. Therefore, it was impossible to go east by traveling west. It wasn't until Columbus shifted the thinking and created a new paradigm that the impossible became possible. More recently, just a few years ago, it was thought to be impossible for the communist-run Soviet Union to be replaced by a group of independent states experimenting with democracy. Again, only after a major shift in thinking did the impossible become possible.

Here's an example that shows the influence of paradigms on one's life. Nancy had been transferred into sales after proving herself in a customer-support role. Customers had truly enjoyed working with her, and this feedback prompted her move. In sales for less than a year, Nancy was quiet and hesitant to speak up during our training course. It was in a one-on-one coaching session that her paradigms began to surface.

Nancy was asked to describe those times in her life that

she had felt successful, but she could not identify any. She had graduated from college with a 3.6 GPA, but she didn't feel successful because it hadn't been a 4.0. Several other situations came up which fit this same pattern. Whatever she did wasn't good enough. This paradigm meant she couldn't speak up to other people because she felt that what she would say would not be important. This paradigm of inadequacy controlled her life, leaving her unsatisfied with any accomplishments, and it dictated her unassertive behavior in all of her relationships.

Once we uncovered this paradigm that controlled her behavior, she saw the results: the pain, the frustration, and the fear. Then she found a strong desire for change. She was asked how a "bold and powerful" Nancy would look, talk, and walk. For over an hour, we worked on the traits that would communicate a more powerful image of her. With each change, she became more excited and more forceful in her communication. Even as soon as the next day, her co-workers could not believe the change in her.

PARADIGM SHIFTS

Understanding the limiting effects of a current paradigm is the first step in deciding to break free. A paradigm shift demands a new way of thinking, a new set of beliefs, and a new set of rules for achieving success. A paradigm shift also opens up new possibilities not previously thought possible.

An obvious example of a paradigm shift is the one Christopher Columbus affected. Often individuals who believe in something outside the current paradigm are considered strange or even crazy. Think of the courage it took for Columbus to convince Queen Isabella to invest in his crazy scheme so that he could recruit a crew to sail three little ships past the edge of the earth.

Columbus proved the world was not flat, so he shifted the existing paradigm. As a result, a new set of beliefs developed to deal with the new reality. History is full of paradigm shifts, and one is occurring right now in the field of sales—a powerful shift that will forever change the way we sell, train people to sell, and manage and motivate people to sell. This new model of selling brings with it a new set of rules for achieving success.

We call the new paradigm of selling the "Synergistic Paradigm." *Synergism,* from the Greek word *sunergos,* meaning "working together," is the collaboration needed between two or more people to achieve an effect greater than the sum of the contributions of each. Or, the whole is greater than the sum of its parts. The selling-buying process is synergistic. No matter how much a seller wants to sell, the process will not work if the buyer is not ready. And a buyer requires that someone sell her what she needs. In other words, both must collaborate to effectively complete the process.

The new paradigm also demands a fundamental change in the relationships between salespeople and their sales managers, and between salespeople and other departments or organizations involved in the sales process. Effective selling today insists on salespeople being able to develop synergistic relationships with anyone who impacts their success. Furthermore, the new paradigm has dramatic implications for the way salespeople are trained as there are new skills and techniques to be learned. The culture must also change to provide consistent support for the new thinking and new behavior of the Synergistic Paradigm. The rules of the new paradigm of sales impact every area of sales today. To avoid any issue is to invite failure.

Let's examine this model of the paradigm shift in selling:

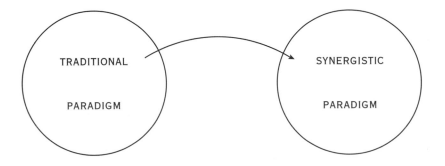

TRADITIONAL

PARADIGM

SYNERGISTIC

PARADIGM

The Traditional Paradigm of selling

* is based on our history, our conditioning from the win-lose culture in which we grew up;
* is comfortable; we know the rules and have adopted strategies, personal ways of behaving, to live and work with others;
* limits our thinking and our actions; we seem to have very little choice; we actually relate to others as if we're on automatic pilot.

The Synergistic Paradigm of selling

* is based on new possibilities; we are not limited to the typical results of our past win-lose conditioning but are free to create a whole new level of sales performance from win-win collaboration with others;
* is uncomfortable for many, because it represents a new game with a new set of rules;
* provides salespeople the ability to get off of automatic pilot, and the freedom to make more choices in their relationships with others.

Even though, as we discovered in chapter 1, the consec quences of the traditional win-lose paradigm are pretty disastrous, it's what we know. The traditional model is comfortable. We know the rules of the game, and everyone has developed their own strategies for playing the game the best they can. These strategies become the automatic pilot that controls our lives and limits our opportunities.

One point that Barker stresses in this book is that "When a new paradigm appears, everyone goes back to zero." In other words, a new game demands new rules; therefore, as the game of selling has changed, so have the rules for success. What made salespeople successful in the past won't work today. Therefore, everyone involved with sales must learn the new rules. This makes it difficult for successful, experienced sales executives. They are more attached to the old paradigm. They know the rules of success in the win-lose paradigm and are very comfortable with them. It is hard for them to let go of their conventional thinking as it is the foundation of their success. But a paradigm shift in the field of sales has occurred, and leadership in the new game will come from those individuals and organizations who learn the new rules of success.

The new Synergistic Paradigm of selling represents a fundamental and pervasive change. This transformation impacts the relationships between sellers and buyers and the relationships between salespeople and their sales managers and between salespeople and internal support departments. It also demands changes in the way salespeople are trained, the organizational culture they work in, the structure of their work teams, and the quota and compensation systems their pay is based on. Quite simply, this new model redefines and revolutionizes the sales profession.

These are dramatic changes requiring a new set of skills and operating principles. New skills become the pathway for people to change old behaviors. Furthermore, individuals and organizations must be willing to take the risks inherent in any change. However, the interesting paradox is that not changing is the real risk. If you keep doing the same thing that we know is ineffective while others are making changes, you are putting yourself and your organization at great risk.

Chapter Summary

1. A paradigm is a model, a pattern of thinking that determines how we perceive our world, thus creating the basis for our reality.
2. Paradigms are invisible and exist below our level of consciousness.
3. Paradigms shape what is possible and what is achievable.
4. Paradigms provide a set of rules for success.

5. A paradigm shift is a transition to a new way of thinking.
6. A paradigm shift is occurring in the field of sales, and with this transformation comes a new set of skills essential for success.

CHAPTER THREE

SELLING

IN THE SYNERGISTIC

PARADIGM

You never "close" a sale, you open a long-term relationship.
—*DENNIS WAITLEY*

The typical relationship between sellers and buyers is based on adversarial positions. In the Traditional Paradigm, selling has always been interpreted as getting the buyer to do something they probably wouldn't do otherwise. This chapter, then, presents a dramatic way for salespeople to change their approach to the seller-buyer relationship.

This new synergistic method works for all types of seller-buyer relationships, from the brief relationship characterized by the one-time transaction to those that involve multiple interactions to consummate the purchase decision. The synergistic method is especially applicable to those permanent, ongoing relationships between the seller and buyer. Let's examine each of those in a little more detail.

The simplest form and first level of selling is the one-time transaction. Here the decision to buy is made in a short period of time. This level includes retail sales, telemarketing sales for long-distance networks and other products and services, office equipment sales, some forms of insurance sales, pre-need funeral arrangements sales, and so on. Salespeople who work in this type of selling usually sell some sort of standardized product.

It's interesting to see how important even the brief relationship has become in many of these industries. A buyer wants the salesperson to listen to her needs, provide suitable options, and help her make a decision without applying pressure. In other words, the buyer wants to buy from a trusted source—she does not want to be sold. So not only is the relationship a critical element of that particular decision-making process, but it is an important factor in building customer satisfaction. This builds a stronger reputation for the salesperson and the organization, so essential to creating repeat business.

Even major areas in the sales profession previously considered to be of the "one-time close" mentality have changed. Most automotive salespeople, once considered by most consumers to be the epitome of the slam-dunk style of selling, now know the value of building strong customer relationships, and successful insurance salespeople build their business from referrals and renewals from their established customer base.

The next level of sales includes those seller-buyer situations that require multiple interactions to consummate the purchasing decision. The higher the price or the more complex the technology, the more interactions that are usually required. It is here that salespeople maintain frequent contact with prospective buyers with the intention of one day making a sale. Selling at this level demands even more ability for building and maintaining long-term relationships.

Products and services are becoming increasingly customized to the buyer's needs, and a closer relationship requiring an increased flow of information back and forth is characteristic at this level. This level also represents a more complex sale. More people are involved in the selling-buying process, and multiple layers of management get involved within organizations. People who sell real estate, health-care programs to organizations, high-tech medical equipment for hospitals, custom computer networking, and so on all sell at this level.

Finally, there is the level of ongoing, permanent seller-buyer relationships that require full "relationship management" skills. Much like a marriage, these situations demand that you break down the walls between yourself and your customer. You know each other's business inside and out. There is a major trend toward this level of selling, especially in the quality movement as many proponents of total quality management believe in the value of a "single-source supplier."

These ongoing relationships can be as simple as the route salesperson continually stocking the shelves of a supermarket and working on merchandising programs which benefit the store to the relationship between wholesale and retail levels of an organization. An example here is the complex relationship between manufacturing companies and their independent distributors such as an automotive manufacturer and its dealers. The new, rapidly growing field of "network marketing" would be included here also. In each case, the success of both parties depends upon the effectiveness of the relationship.

The term "partnership" has become more popular recently to describe this ongoing relationship between buyers and sellers. Yet in our experience, most organizations throw the word around in sales meetings without much knowledge as to what it really means. Nor are salespeople taught the skills to create this kind of a relationship with their customers. For example, how can a manufacturing organization continue to make unilateral marketing decisions without including their distributors and call it a partnership?

The *American Heritage Dictionary* defines *partnership* as "the state of being in relationship with somebody in which each has equal status and a certain independence but with certain implicit or formal obligations to each other." Equal status! That doesn't work for the manufacturing company that believes their distributors are lucky to be selected to carry their product. Obligations to each other! That too doesn't hold much water when the parent company thinks they can constantly ship orders to their distributors with "on back order" appearing frequently next to ordered items. Yet they sure spend a lot of time talking about the partnerships with their distributors at company meetings.

Partnership is actually the foundation of the Synergistic Paradigm. It is the context in which the seller-buyer relationship flourishes. Being in partnership is something you are, not something you do. And it can show up at all three levels of selling.

Let's examine the four characteristics of partnership that apply to salespeople and their organizations as well.

First, partnerships have an interdependent nature to them. Being in partnership with someone means first of all you know you cannot, or choose not to, do it on your own. You realize that each is dependent on the other to get the desired results. This is usually the understanding people have when they utilize the word partnership to define their relationship with another. But more is needed to create a true partnership.

The second characteristic is that you must be committed to your partner getting her needs met. In other words, you must live from a commitment to win/win relationships. And it's actually deeper than that. Partnership evolves when providing for the other person is something you *enjoy* doing; when service to others, contributing to others, and making a difference in others' lives is simply who you are. Again, it's a way of being, not necessarily techniques you are trained to use.

A commitment to produce a result bigger than the individuals in the partnership is the third characteristic of being in partnership. In other words, in the interaction between a seller and buyer in partnership, there is a bigger commitment in the background, something that keeps them working together. For example, Barbara is a sales executive for a printing company that specializes in producing custom presentation binders for their customers. When she creates a partnership with a client, the actual seller-buyer interactions are included under a bigger commitment. In Barbara's situation, it may be the commitment she and her clients have to improve the quality of communication of corporate values and products to others. So when she and her clients work together on specific projects, they are working on producing results bigger than the individual project.

The fourth characteristic is that partnerships have a future. A partnership is larger in scope than a single deal, or a one-time seller-buyer transaction. Being in partnership means there is ongoing communication and therefore the possibility of continuous growth and improvement. The partnership becomes the basis for constantly looking for new ways to improve the seller's products and the buyer's use of those products, thereby maximizing the effectiveness of the partnership and the value of being in partnership.

The three levels of seller-buyer interactions discussed earlier represent different circumstances, not methods of selling. The state of being in partnership can be brought to any of the levels. It's your choice whether you want the interactions with your customers to occur in the context of the Traditional Paradigm of selling or in the context of partnership, the foundation of the Synergistic Paradigm.

The following chart will help you distinguish between the sales approach in the Traditional Paradigm of selling and the Synergistic Paradigm.

Traditional Paradigm vs. Synergistic Paradigm

Buyers are seen as malleable, controllable, able to be manipulated or controlled if only the Seller finds the right gimmick or canned message.	*Buyers are seen as self-directing, capable of assuming responsibility for their own decisions.*
Seller wants to use information about Buyers or "techniques" to get them to reach a decision already determined by the Seller.	*Seller wants to help Buyers reach a decision of their own choosing based on the buyer's needs and wants.*

Seller employs strategies, appropriate phrases, and clever tactics with the goal of pushing the selling process from "opening" to the "close" as fast as possible.	*Seller is a facilitator—helping the Buyer move through the buying process step by step until they reach a decision. Thus, there is no selling process imposed on the Buyer.*
Seller diagnoses Buyer's "style," "typology," "traits," "position on a grid," their "personality type."	*Seller avoids stereotyping or diagnosing Buyer. Instead, Seller concentrates on understanding only what Buyers are saying or doing.*
By "diagnosing" the style of Buyers, the clever salesperson chooses the right methods for controlling them—knowing what buttons to push.	*Seller avoids trying to control or direct Buyers. Instead Seller tries to accept where Buyers are in the buying process and what they need in each stage of that process.*
The language of control is used: i.e., probing, overcoming objections, using closing strategies, bringing the Buyer forward, using leading questions to get yes answers, handling stalls, and so on.	*The language of collaborating and facilitating is used: helping Buyers find a solution that will meet their needs, helping them through their decision-making process, being a consultant.*

As you can see, this point-by-point contrast reflects the dramatic shift in our thinking about the seller-buyer relationship. For many people, the ways of synergism seem strange and uncomfortable, as does anything outside our normal realm. Consequently, there is a tendency to disregard or ignore it, or rationalize our way around it. To do so, however, limits our ability to learn.

A popular motivational poster has this message: "The mind, like a parachute, functions only when open." Keep your mind open during this chapter as we identify five key principles of selling in the Synergistic Paradigm. They are straightforward and easy to understand. To benefit from them, one must first believe in their validity and, second, commit to applying them in sales.

Here are the five basic operating principles of selling in the Synergistic Paradigm:

1. Abandon any system of "selling steps." Because buyers make the final decision, they go through a set of "buying steps."
2. Control and pressure create resistance and obstacles to the normal flow of the buying process.
3. Salespeople must create an atmosphere conducive to the buyer moving toward a decision whether to buy or not.
4. Salespeople must see themselves as consultants.
5. Salespeople must create value.

Again, these five principles apply to all sales situations, from one-time transactions, to those that include multiple interactions to consummate the purchasing decision, and finally to the ongoing, permanent relationship between sellers and buyers.

ABANDON THE STEPS OF THE SELLING PROCESS

The traditional model of selling is based on a series of hypothetical selling steps—opening, probing, presenting, handling objections, and closing, or some similar variation. This sequence is designed to provide a structure for the salesperson to control the call. More control is supposed to mean more power over the other person and thus more success in selling. As we have said before, selling has always been analogous to a chess game: the person who implements the best strategy wins. The traditional thinking is to teach a salesperson a series of steps and the skills to carefully manipulate buyers through those steps. Unfortunately, this thinking doesn't take into consideration that the buyers on the other side of the desk have their own needs. That's why the traditional selling process is actually detrimental to sales success.

Buyers ultimately make the purchasing decision, and they want to participate actively in reaching that decision. Anytime a buyer makes a decision to buy something, she follows a series of steps. There is a logical sequence of steps that people go through, usually without being aware of it, when they make any decision in their lives—from buying a car to deciding where to go grocery shopping to selecting a vacation. Our objective here is to highlight the buying steps so that salespeople are able to sense where their buyers are in the process at any given time.

Selling successfully in the Synergistic Paradigm requires constant awareness of the buyer's own decision-making process. The role of the salesperson is to facilitate the buyer's going through six steps of this process and making sure that it is unfolding naturally. The six steps are

1. identify and define buyer's unmet needs or fears;
2. generate alternative solutions;
3. examine and evaluate the alternative solutions;
4. decide on the best solution(s);
5. implement the decision;
6. evaluate the outcomes.

Let's walk together as buyers through the process. Assume that we want to buy a car.

At Step 1, we try to identify our unmet needs or fears. We need a four-door to replace our old two-door. We want to buy an American-made car at this time, yet we are afraid of low quality. We need a car that gets good gas mileage. We fear the costs of a high interest rate. We need more trunk space. We wonder whether it would be economical to drive the old car another year. We may even have some priority established as to what needs we would give up and what needs we wouldn't.

At Step 2, we consider different alternatives that will satisfy our needs. That could mean going to several dealerships, looking at the different models, or if our needs are more specific, we might just go to a specific dealer and look at the different models available there. The main point is that we are still in Step 2, considering alternatives. It is here that many automobile salespeople fail. They want to push us to the next steps, Step 3 (examining and evaluating alternatives) and Step 4 (determining the best solution), before we are ready and thus create resistance to the sale. If the salesperson just shows what's available (Step 2), she will avoid most sales resistance.

At Step 3, we examine and evaluate our alternatives. We test-drive the car, negotiate price, listen to the sales pitch and whatever else to get all the information we can to make the decision. We also judge the quality and credibility of the information the salesperson is providing us. This can be a very tedious step for some people and a spontaneous one for others. Salespeople have to be alert to the process of each buyer.

At Step 4 we make the decision. Some people say it's not that easy. But remember, in Step 3 we did a lot of evaluating to get to the decision. Step 4 is committing oneself to the decision: "This is what I've decided to do."

At Step 5 we determine what we have to do to implement our decision. In our automobile example, this is when we sign the papers, arrange our financing, or whatever else needs to be done.

At Step 6 we evaluate our buying decision—usually later. Does the new car fit our needs and expectations? We usually evaluate one other critical element at Step 6—*how we were treated during the process by the salesperson.*

The key is that buyers, like most people, want to make their own decisions. When we feel someone is trying to push us, we get resistant and resentful. Salespeople need what psychologists call "respect for the self-determining nature of human beings." Buyers want to have the opportunity to make their own decision without coercion. The traditional sales model puts the salesperson in control. It's logical, then, that potential buyers usually revert to defense mechanisms—fight, flight, or submit. In the traditional sales model, buyer resistance is regarded as an obstacle to overcome. Salespeople's attempts at control not only create additional resistance, but are self-defeating to the process and, inevitably, damaging to the relationship.

The salesperson's role is to facilitate the process. To facilitate means to free the buyer from difficulties and obstacles, to make the process easier and to assist in the decision making. The traditional sales steps actually impede the buying process. They make the salesperson's agenda the priority and generally confuse the issue. The message to salespeople here is "Get out of your own way."

Obviously, there is no script for the salesperson to follow in this process. This is of critical importance. In the Synergistic Paradigm, the script to follow is the buyer's lead through her decision-making process.

Also there is no typecasting for the salesperson to use—no need to try to figure out the buyer's type, which quadrant he falls in, what mode of thinking he uses. Each human being has a unique set of needs and different perceptions of the best way to satisfy those needs. In the Synergistic Paradigm, it's more important to focus on the buyer's communication than on their personality type. In addition, typecasting a buyer will set up predetermined beliefs that will actually limit the relationship. Your behavior will be tainted and distorted by the typecasting.

A participant in a training session of ours shared this example. She was calling on the vice president of sales of a client's organization. It was her first meeting with him, and she was escorted into a nice big office that reeked of "power." Everything showed signs of a "driver, results-oriented" personality, and having just completed such a sales-training course, she was ready to get to the bottom line. She started talking about the results her product would provide the organization, and her client kept changing the subject. After much effort, she finally gave up and let the client determine the flow of the call.

On the way out of the office, she complimented her client on his office and he replied that it wasn't his. He told her that his office was such a mess he borrowed his boss's office for their meeting. As she discovered later, his boss was a perfectionist. His wife had, in fact, decorated the office. After our course, she vowed to focus on what her customers were saying instead of trying to read their personality.

The six steps of the buyer's decision-making process apply to all levels of selling. A buyer may go through these steps in one interaction with a salesperson, or he may take many months or even years to go through the process for large complex deals. In other situations, other individuals who influence the buying decision may be involved at particular steps in the process. In an ongoing partnership between buyer and seller, there are many individual cycles of the process. The point is, anytime a buyer is in the process of making any decision, he goes through these six steps.

Once again, success in the new selling paradigm requires a sensitivity to letting people make their own decisions. This means letting go of the seller-controlled process and facilitating the decision-making process for the buyer. This yields greater results and more effective decisions for both the buyer and the seller.

CONTROL AND PRESSURE CREATE RESISTANCE

The more I try to get you to do what I want you to do, the less chance of success I will have. Buyers want to make their decisions freely. Pressure creates resistance. Resistance in turn generates more pressure and so on. The more sales pressure we put on someone, the more buyer resistance we are creating.

We even cause people to resist decisions that are to their advantage because they are feeling coerced. Resistance is a red flag that something is wrong in the process. Stop whatever you are doing and listen to the cause of the resistance.

Here's an example of the typical pressure-resistance-pressure cycle in a one-time transaction situation. The buyer answers the phone at home after dinner.

BUYER: Hello.

SELLER: Hello, Mr. Johnson, my name is Ms. Abbott with the Telstar long-distance network, and I'd like to tell you about our new pricing plan. Which service are you currently using?

BUYER: Well, Ms. Abbott, we're using Galactic, and we're very pleased with the service.

SELLER: I understand you're pleased with the existing service, but we have a new plan that could save you a lot of money. How much do you spend on long distance now?

BUYER: Look, I said we're very happy with Galactic. We've used their service for years and don't feel a need to change.

SELLER: But Mr. Johnson, if I could show you how you could save twenty percent on your long distance service would you be interested?

BUYER: No, I wouldn't, and anyway, I don't believe any of the numbers you all throw around. Everyone's got some gimmick or another. So, no thank you.

SELLER: Well, I understand, but just give me a moment and I'll explain how our billing works.

BUYER: No! I said I'm not interested!

SELLER: You mean you don't want to save any money?

BUYER: Good-bye! (hangs up)

Nothing was gained at all in continuing to push and a lot was lost. If at some time in the future, Johnson decides to consider an alternative long-distance network, you can bet Telstar won't be on his list.

Remember the kid's toy with different-shaped holes and blocks that fit the holes? There was a round hole, a square, a rectangle, a triangle, a star, a plus sign, a hexagon, and so forth. Matching your product and services to buyers' needs is much like fitting the blocks into the correct hole. If it fits, it goes right in. If it doesn't, no amount of work and effort will make it fit. Watch a child trying to fit the triangle-shaped block into the star-shaped hole and a salesperson pressuring his product on his customer when it doesn't fit her needs. The reactions are pretty similar—a lot of frustration. The problem is that the child usually learns more quickly!

To return to salespeople pressuring customers, it's the same story over and over again. Apply pressure, no results; apply more pressure, still no results. In fact, buyers and others can be put in the position of defending something they don't totally believe just to resist the pressure being exerted on them.

For example, let's assume John and Cindy are having lunch and discussing a controversial issue such as gun control. John is opposed to gun control and laughs at some remark a local senator made during an interview. He asks Cindy what she believes, and she responds that she doesn't know much about it, but that she is probably for gun control because of the deaths caused by gunshots. John says, "That's a ridiculous argument" that guns don't kill people, people do. Cindy feels pushed to defend her beliefs, and John has a counter for her every response. The more he pushes, the more she defends her beliefs, and the stronger her beliefs become. By the time they're through with lunch, she has no doubt about her position on gun control.

The effective salesperson is not necessarily one that overcomes resistance but one that prevents it in the first place.

SALESPEOPLE MUST ESTABLISH AN ATMOSPHERE CONDUCIVE TO DECISION MAKING

The decision-making process involves the possibility of change. That means leaving something that is comfortable and familiar in favor of something unknown. Almost any change in life creates feelings of uncertainty and doubt. Salespeople must establish a relationship with buyers in which these feelings can be discussed—an atmosphere conducive to change.

Kurt Lewin, a psychologist who researched how people change, has said: "Before an innovation [change] is accepted, there must occur an unfreezing of the changee's present belief system. This unfreezing will be facilitated when the changee has the opportunity to openly express his loyalty and allegiance to the old beliefs and the fear and doubt of changing beliefs."

Change entails both: allegiance to the old way and fear and doubt about the new. Customers and clients need an opportunity to talk openly about their concerns. As a result, the salesperson must be skilled in nonjudgmental listening. Only then will customers feel comfortable raising these questions. In the traditional model of selling, these questions are considered "objections to overcome." This conveys to the customer the message either that their feelings about change are wrong or that you have all the answers about what they should do. It stifles the flow of open, honest communication necessary for building synergistic partnerships.

In the traditional model, sellers talk a lot and show their knowledge. Salespeople have been programmed to believe that overcoming buyers' objections is a crucial element of the sale. It's difficult for them to understand the importance of just listening to these concerns and not taking action to "overcome them."

So often, once these feelings of doubt are brought to the surface and treated as valid, their power to impede the change process goes away. But when they never surface, or when they are brought up and denied, they have the power to sabotage the relationship. Here's an example of how a salesperson might deal with these feelings of doubt in the traditional model. This exchange takes place in an automotive dealership:

BUYER: Jim, I really appreciate your time, but I think I'll stick with my old car just a little longer. It seems like a lot of money to commit right now.

SELLER: Okay, Marsha, it's your decision, but you have to realize our sale is over tomorrow and you'll never find a deal like this again.

BUYER: Well, I just don't know. I just moved and I'm paying more in rent and I've got a lot of bills.

SELLER: Don't worry about it. You told me you've got a promotion coming up. You'll be in good shape.

BUYER: Yeah, but you can't count on those things. Besides, this seems a little extravagant. The car I have runs fine.

SELLER: Marsha, look, that car has a lot of miles on it. It won't be long before it starts bleeding you dry with repairs. Anyway, you deserve some fun in your life. This new car is just what you need.

BUYER: No, it isn't just what I need.

SELLER: Look, I'll make you a deal. If you take the car today, I'll throw in a CD player at no cost.

BUYER: Jim, I don't want a CD player, and I don't want a new car. I'm just fine with my old one.

Jim had a response to every one of Marsha's concerns. That's what we do when we see the buyer as an obstacle to our winning the chess game. We have to prove to the buyer why buying the car is the right thing to do. Now let's look at the same situation. This time, however, Jim will listen to Marsha's allegiance to the old and her doubt about the change. He will create an atmosphere that allows her to address her own issues.

BUYER: Jim, I really appreciate your time, but I think I'll stick with my old car just a little longer. It seems like a lot of money to commit right now.

SELLER: It sounds like you're a little hesitant to make the financial commitment, especially since your present car is running just fine.

BUYER: Yeah, that's true. I've just moved and my rent is higher, so maybe I should be a little conservative.

SELLER: Okay, so you're feeling a need to be a little cautious.

BUYER: Yeah, that's right, but the other side of me says I really deserve a new car. I've been working real hard and

my promotion looks pretty certain. Plus, I'm getting concerned about the miles I have on my existing car and the
possible repair costs facing me.

SELLER: So even though you feel good about your promotion,
you're concerned about moving to a nicer apartment and
getting a new car at the same time. And you really like
your old car, but you're worried about it starting to need
some repairs. Is there anything I can do to help?

BUYER: Well, you know what, there is. Can we go back over
the financing options? I've got a couple of additional
questions.

Notice how much smoother the process is in the second
example. In this scenario, Jim is able to help Marsha address
her buying concerns by just listening to her concerns and not
"selling" against them. This attitude has a major impact on
the quality of the seller-buyer relationship.

By demonstrating your understanding of what the buyer
must go through to change, you are establishing an environment more conducive to that change.

SALESPEOPLE MUST SEE THEMSELVES
AS CONSULTANTS

A consultant is a person, usually with no authority, who relies
solely on her influence derived from knowledge and expertise
to help individuals or organizations "buy" new ways of doing
things. How that knowledge and expertise are shared,
though, is the critical factor. The principal difference between
a knowledgeable consultant and a know-it-all sales rep is how
the information is shared.

Here's a thought from our seminars: *If you have a product or service that will benefit me or my organization, you
must inform me in a responsible fashion so that I am open to
your information.*

Whatever products or services you sell, you are a consultant to your clients. You are an individual with knowledge and expertise that might benefit your clients. Let's look at what successful consultants do. First of all, they make sure they are hired by the client before offering their expertise. Then they make sure the client perceives a problem or unmet need before offering their expertise. At the same time, they make sure that they, too, understand the problem or unmet need.

Once this has been accomplished, they let the client remain in charge of the decision-making process. They listen to and acknowledge the client's resistance to change. They make sure they have correct facts and figures or know how to get them. Finally, they leave the responsibility with the client for buying or accepting their knowledge. They don't hassle or pressure the client.

A consultant knows her role is more than selling a product or service. Many times she must provide knowledge and experience in other areas that support the use of the product or service. Judy, now a product marketing manager for one of the country's largest telecommunication companies, remembers this experience while she was a district sales manager.

One of her account executives and a technical support person met with the president of a bank computer company. The client organization was very dependent on data transmission, and they were having some problems. Instead of listening to the client, Judy's people got defensive and blamed much of the problem on the poor technical training the client's employees received. The president threw them out of his office.

Judy called the president and went over to his office to apologize. After listening to his problems, she offered to bring a small team of people in to analyze the situation and help in determining the organization's overall goals and direction (the first step in a consultant's process—analyze the situation). Once the initial survey was complete, she considered all of the options available to her client (the second step in the consultant's process—consider alternatives). She then developed and recommended a full plan on how the bank computer company could not only correct the existing problems, but also market their services more effectively to their clients (the third step in a consultant's process—make recommendations). The system justification she provided motivated the president to buy the whole package (the fourth step in a consultant's process—motivate to action by providing value). The decision proved to be very beneficial to the bank computer company and to her organization as she consummated a very large data transmission sale.

Consultants analyze the situation, consider alternatives, make recommendations, and motivate clients to action by providing value. Like a doctor who recommends surgery without a thorough analysis of the patient's condition, a salesperson recommending a product or service without understanding the client's situation is guilty of malpractice.

Successful salespeople in the new Synergistic Paradigm see themselves as consultants. They know their sales success depends upon their ability to share their expertise in a responsible manner that contributes to their clients.

SALESPEOPLE MUST CREATE VALUE

Buyers buy value, not price. If your buyer informs you that he is going with a competitor who quoted a cheaper price, he is telling you that he does not see enough difference, in things that are important to him, to substantiate the difference in price. The decision to buy is always based on the buyer's perception of what will this do for me versus what do I have to give up for it (pay for it, in most cases). In other words, a buyer will only buy the product or service that is worth more to him than what he must pay for it: the product or service that provides value, or that provides the best value in a competitive situation.

Nestled away in a great little book published in 1965, *The New Psychology of Persuasion and Motivation in Selling*, is a formula the authors (Whitney, Hubin, and Murphy) developed to reflect "value." They asserted that economic value could be represented by this formula:

$$\text{Economic Value} = \frac{\text{Quality + Utility + Service}}{\text{Price}}$$

Notice that "Economic Value" can only be increased by increasing the numerator (Quality + Utility (how I use it) + Service) or decreasing the denominator (Price). The key to this formula is to remember that the terms *quality, utility,* and *service* means the buyer's perception, not yours. What you or your company think is important may not be important to your buyer at all. Therefore, it's essential that you ask questions and listen to learn the factors important to the buyer in determining his perception of these qualities— quality, utility, and service.

The important thing to remember here is that when your competitor starts cutting prices, you may not need to do the same just to stay in the ball game. By improving the buyer's perception of the numerator, you can improve the Economic Value ratio and not decrease the denominator at all.

Chapter Summary

1. The three primary types of seller-buyer relationships are
   - the one-time transaction
   - multiple interactions to consummate the purchasing decision
   - the ongoing, long-term relationship
2. Partnership is the foundation of the Synergistic Paradigm. It is the context in which all types of seller-buyer relationships flourish.
3. Partnership is a state of being, not something you do. There are four basic characteristics of being in partnership.

- Partnerships are interdependent in nature.
- Partnership evolves when you are committed to your partner getting her needs met, and when providing for, servicing, and contributing to the other person is something you enjoy doing.
- Partnership means being committed to something bigger than the individuals.
- Partnerships have a future beyond a single deal or a one-time transaction.

4. The five basic operating principles of the Synergistic Paradigm are:
   - Abandon any system of selling steps.
   - Control and pressure create resistance and obstacles to the normal flow of the buying process.
   - Salespeople must establish an atmosphere conducive to change.
   - Salespeople must see themselves as consultants.
   - Salespeople must create value.

5. The six steps to the Buyer's Decision-Making process are:
   - identify and define unmet needs and fears
   - generate alternative solutions
   - examine and evaluate the alternatives
   - decide on best solution
   - implement the decision
   - evaluate the outcomes

6. The more you try to control the behavior of another person, the less influence you have in that relationship.

7. For people to change their attitudes, behaviors, and beliefs, they must have an opportunity to express their allegiance to the old and their fear and doubt about the new.

8. A consultant is a person, usually with no authority, who relies solely on her influence to help individuals and organizations buy new ways of doing things.

9. Economic Value, the basis for all buying decisions, is defined by this formula:

$$\text{Economic Value} = \frac{\text{Quality} + \text{Utility} + \text{Service}}{\text{Price}}$$

CHAPTER FOUR

HOW TO LISTEN

MORE EFFECTIVELY TO

BUYERS AND OTHERS

To be with another in this way means, that for the time being, you lay aside your own views and values in order to enter another's world without prejudice.

—*CARL ROGERS*

To implement the five operating principles for selling in the Synergistic Paradigm successfully, you must first learn to listen. You probably know from your personal life that people have a deep need to have someone listen to them. This is at the very essence of human behavior. When people feel they are being heard, they respond favorably to the listener, and new possibilities open up in their relationship.

Our concept of listening consists of more than just the physical activity. We mean interpreting and understanding the message, in its entirety, without imposing our preconceived ideas or opinions. This listening is an active mental process requiring practice and development. You have to understand more than the words spoken and get to the heart of the matter by sensing what's not being said.

Ninety-five percent of the participants in our course tell us that they thought they were good listeners before our program. The course, though, opens up a whole new dimension in what listening to their buyers and others is really like. As a result, participants leave with a much broader understanding and a higher skill level of this critical communication tool. From this experience, we know that many of you have begun reading this chapter thinking: "I am already a good listener."

Perhaps we should start by using an example. Volkswagen recently created a new advertising campaign based on "Fahrvergnügen." The campaign is designed to stimulate a new image for their cars. They get your attention with a unique new word and then create a new feeling for the word throughout the commercial. They, in fact, create a new word to identify a new experience. The objective is to get the viewer to differentiate between driving a Volkswagen and driving another car. Our goal here is the same: to get you to differentiate between your existing concept of listening and the level of listening we are going to address.

Many innovative leaders in the field of interpersonal communication have been teaching the value of listening for decades. Co-author Tom Gordon was one of the first to recognize the importance of listening to the seller-buyer relationship. In a 1959 speech to the Sales and Marketing Executives National Convention, he said:

> What this approach [listening] will do is to satisfy some of the basic needs of the customer—his needs to feel listened to, understood, accepted, and respected, and his very strong need to be self-directing, self-determining and self-responsible. . . . Might it be that this new sales approach will find sales executives, in the future, becoming less con-

cerned about the "sales pitch" and more concerned about the "sales catch"?

In the Synergistic Paradigm, listening is a skill used to understand and accept the buyer's perception of the world. This is done for one reason only—to understand and accept the buyer's perception of the world. This represents a significant shift from the role of listening in the Traditional Paradigm. There salespeople are taught listening skills for the purpose of getting the right information to load their presentation gun. In other words, listening is taught as asking the proper questions to determine the buyer's needs on which you then base your presentation. In many sales courses, it's called "probing." In the Synergistic Paradigm, listening is not a skill used on the buyer; listening is a way of understanding the buyer.

To understand and accept the buyer's views, needs, and concerns means appreciating their apprehension, their doubts, their fears and anxiety over the decision. It includes looking at the world from their side of the desk and understanding, among other things, their disappointment and frustration when you don't deliver as promised. Furthermore, it means feeling their embarrassment when others second-guess their decision. Your opinions, judgments, or excuses have to be set aside in order to gain this degree of understanding about their point of view.

You want to create an environment in which the buyers feel safe in voicing concerns so that they can make the best decision possible. At the same time that you suspend judging or evaluating, you have to avoid responding defensively to an "objection" or aggressively to a "buying signal." The buyer must feel you care about perceptions, that you want to understand views and concerns.

As noted earlier, listening in this form must be developed and practiced. In this chapter, we are going to look at what blocks effective listening and then list the characteristics of an effective listener. In the next chapter, we'll show you the application of the listening skills to three vital areas of the seller-buyer relationship: listening to the buyer's needs, listening to his resistance to change, and listening to upset customers.

WHY AREN'T WE BETTER LISTENERS?

There are four major reasons for not being more effective in our listening to others:

1. We didn't learn how to listen.
2. We believe that selling is talking.
3. Listening requires focused concentration.
4. Our paradigms distort what we hear.

Let's look at how each of these obstacles affects our ability to listen and understand the views of our buyers, our clients, and others.

WE DIDN'T LEARN HOW TO LISTEN

In his book *Are You Listening?* Dr. Ralph Nichols summarizes research on the communication process. Here's the breakdown of how we spend our time communicating: 9 percent writing, 16 percent reading, 35 percent talking, and 40 percent listening.

Even before we enter school, our parents are working with us to develop our writing, reading, and speaking skills. Then throughout our entire education we take course after course to sharpen those basic skills. Courses in listening, however, are usually part of an advanced degree in communications or psychology. That's a sad statement considering the amount of research now available on the value of listening in building effective relationships.

In addition, few individuals grow up in a family environment with a good listener as a role model. All of our lives we have received positive feedback when we've said the right thing or shown our wisdom through something we've said. Rarely, however, do we get complimented on our listening skills. So when participants get into sales role plays in the course, they have difficulty letting go of past conditioning in favor of just listening to the buyer. The skills of being an effective listener are, in fact, part of a new technology. It wasn't until the late 1950s and early 1960s that researchers investigated the value of listening and the characteristics of effective listening. Even now this critical element of our relationships with others is usually overlooked.

WE BELIEVE THAT SELLING IS TALKING

The basic rule of success in the traditional model of selling is that a good salesperson has a glib tongue and can maintain control of the conversation. Typically, sales training has been based on what you say and how you say it. The stress is on the smooth presentation, the logical way to overcome objections, and the power close.

Participants in our Synergistic Selling course have difficulty overcoming this previous programming. This is especially evident in a two-step exercise created to drive home this point. In the first role play, the participant is asked to simply listen to a friend who wants to get in better shape physically. The listener has no agenda, nothing to sell, no preconceived outcome. Because of this, she makes a reasonable attempt to apply the new listening skills. In the second step of the exercise, we ask the participant to again listen to her friend who wants to get in better physical shape. This time, however, we give the listener an objective, a predetermined outcome such as to convince (to sell) your friend on a piece of home gym equipment. The results are amazing. Immediately, all listening stops and the "seller" takes control of the conversation to lead her friend to her predetermined outcome. And you should see the resistance from the friend. It is a beautiful demonstration of the key principles of selling in the Synergistic Paradigm and the conventional belief that "selling" requires the powers of persuasion.

LISTENING REQUIRES FOCUSED CONCENTRATION

Most people have difficulty concentrating. In fact, we take pride in doing many things at the same time, which actually prohibits concentration. You are probably aware that the average person can think four to five times faster than she can speak. That means we have the mental capacity to think about more than one thing at a time, and many people do just that while someone else is speaking. We do all kinds of things—planning what we are going to say next, thinking about tomorrow's meeting with our boss, evaluating what the speaker is wearing or saying, determining whether we agree with her opinions or not.

Unfortunately, salespeople often listen with a strategy in mind. They selectively listen for information that they want to hear to make the sale. If the buying signals they are looking for don't occur, they ask probing questions to get to the information they want. All the while their mind is focused on their strategy, and they miss opportunity after opportunity to understand where the buyer is in his decision-making process.

Salespeople may also be concentrating on what they need to say next to control the conversation, or to prepare their rebuttal to what the buyer is saying. They consider which questions would elicit the information needed to make their strategy successful. To them the seller-buyer relationship is a chess game, and they are almost always planning their next move or modifying their strategy while the buyer is talking.

If this isn't enough, people are always judging and evaluating what another person is saying. We hear a statement and then judge it to be right or wrong. Think for a moment: how much of your conversation tells people how you agree or disagree with them, rather than just understanding and accepting what they believe.

OUR PARADIGMS DISTORT WHAT WE HEAR

Our past forms paradigms which are the filters through which we experience life. We bring our past experiences into each new conversation. Even if we're meeting an individual for the first time, we bring our history of similar situations. This provides a predetermined set of filters to our listening that often distorts the other person's message. The echoes of our past drown out what is being said in the present.

Here's an example from one of our participants to illustrate this problem:

Recently, I was helping a friend move into a new house, and while we were standing in the garage, she said, "I'll call Bill [her stepfather] and get him to come put up some shelves for us." That was a perfectly innocent statement considering Bill is quite a handyman and has done a lot of work for her in the past. However, all of my life I have been *told* that I am not a good handyman, and I'm not. Frankly, I am envious of those who are. Because of my previous experience on this issue, when she said, "I'll call Bill and get him to come put up some shelves for us," what I heard was: "Since you're not good at fixing things, I'd better call Bill to come over and do this." And I got upset with her for criticizing me! My filters distorted the entire meaning of her communication.

Here is another example in a business context. In one of our recent seminars, a young woman complained about the tone of voice her manager used to communicate with her. When asked what it was she didn't like, without hesitation she replied, "She sounds just like my mother talking to me when I was two years old!" Again, because her manager's tone of voice reminded her of her mother, it interfered with her ability to listen to what was being said.

In every interaction you have with a buyer, all of your past experiences with buyers affects the communication process. Your beliefs about the buyer's sex, race, the clothes they are wearing, and even their title affects how you hear what they say. So the key is to realize how your predetermined set of filters affects the present situation. This awareness will help free you of its control.

THE SKILLS OF AN EFFECTIVE LISTENER

Remember our seminar participants who thought they were good listeners? During our training, they learn new lessons in what an effective listener really is. Perhaps the easiest way to address the listening skills is to break them into three components: attending behavior, passive listening, and active listening.

ATTENDING BEHAVIOR

Attending behavior consists of the nonverbal communications that show the other person that you care about what they are saying. This includes primarily maintaining direct eye contact and an open body posture. Although these body-language techniques are quite simple, they have great impact on the person talking. Everyone has experienced the frustration of talking to someone who is working on something at their desk, observing others in the office, or reading a report. The odd thing is that openly paying attention is often overlooked by the listener, damaging the communication process.

PASSIVE LISTENING

This includes the skills of silence, acknowledgments, and door openers. Let's examine each in turn.

SILENCE. This is fundamentally important: if you are talking, the other person can't. In itself silence can be a very powerful tool because it (1) shows attention to the speaker, (2) avoids any judgmental or defensive responses, and (3) creates mild pressure for the speaker to keep on talking.

   The best times to remain silent are either when the other

person is communicating a steady stream of thoughts and feelings or when the other person seems deep in thought or experiencing a strong emotion. For example, when people pause to reflect on some point, a good listener remains silent and "waits out" the pause rather than interrupting the other person's thoughts.

Take this story: Bob, a very successful advertising salesperson for a national magazine, was a talker, a good presenter, who was very successful in the old paradigm. Even though he didn't seem to pick up much in listening skills during the course, he called two days after the conclusion of the course and told of a meeting that morning with a client.

Several times during the meeting, when he would have normally jumped in and shared his wisdom and expertise, he simply bit his tongue. This allowed the conversation around the table to continue, and several people contributed more than they had before. In the process, new information came to the surface. On the way out the door, the vice president put his arm around Bob's shoulders and said, "Bob, I think I speak for my staff when I say you really listened to us this morning. I think we will give your magazine a chance." Just from biting his tongue!

ACKNOWLEDGMENT. An excellent way of encouraging conversation is simply to acknowledge it. This includes actions like head nodding and leaning forward, or expressions like "uh-huh," "I see," "yes," "mm-hmm," "really," or "how about that." Such acknowledgments let the other person know not only that you are listening but that you care about what you are hearing. Equally important, you avoid evaluating what is being said. For this reason, responses like "That's good," "Excellent," and "You're right" should be avoided.

DOOR OPENERS. As the term implies, these are listener responses that invite the customer to open up to talk about their needs, wants, and concerns. Effective door openers include expressions such as:

"Tell me more about that."
"Help me understand what you are saying."
"I'm interested to hear what you've got to say about that."
"I'd like to hear what you feel about . . ."

Door openers allow the conversation to keep flowing. They are *not* leading questions. Inquiries that solicit a specific response lead the conversation away from the buyer's needs to the seller's needs. For example, questions that begin with "Don't you think that . . ." or "Wouldn't you like to . . ." are often perceived by the buyer as manipulative, and suddenly you've harmed the flow of communication.

ACTIVE LISTENING

Passive listening by itself, though, will only partly achieve your new goals. There is a further level of listening that will ensure you know exactly what the buyer is asking of you. This is called "active listening." To understand this skill, let's turn to the way in which all human communication takes place—the dynamics that are involved when one person attempts to send a message to another. Let a circle represent the buyer who has a need to send a message.

The buyer needs to send a message; something is going on internally. He wants to communicate some feeling, or feel-

BUYER

UPSET

OVER LATE

DELIVERIES

ings, that he is experiencing. In this example, the buyer is upset over late deliveries.

Often the buyer does not directly express what is wrong
but selects a message that represents his feelings and/or
needs. This is the encoding process.

ENCODING

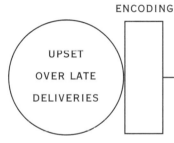

UPSET

OVER LATE

DELIVERIES

"YOU GUYS SURE DON'T WANT MY
BUSINESS VERY MUCH, DO YOU?"

It is important to remember that all coded messages have
two parts—the verbal (the words) and the nonverbal (voice
tone, facial expressions, or posture). Furthermore, most messages contain two types of information: the person's thoughts,
ideas, knowledge, or data (the facts), and the person's emotions, attitudes, sentiments, and values (the feelings) associated with those facts. The careful listener must tune in to both
of these elements to achieve true understanding.

Once a message has been communicated, the receiver
must decode it in an effort to understand what is going on.

In this case, anybody might correctly "decode" the
buyer's message: "He sounds upset." But if the listener does

"YOU GUYS SURE DON'T WANT MY BUSINESS VERY MUCH, DO YOU?"

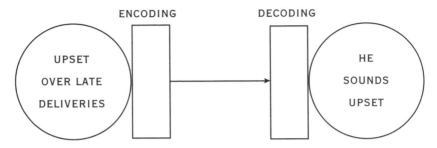

not communicate this impression to the buyer, the buyer does not know for sure that he has been heard. What active listening does is "close the loop" in communication, providing the buyer feedback. The active listener shares her impression of what has been said.

"YOU GUYS SURE DON'T WANT MY BUSINESS VERY MUCH, DO YOU?"

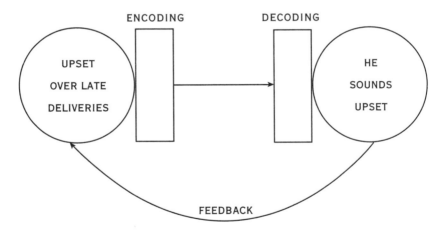

"YOU SOUND UPSET WITH US."

The buyer now has a chance to express even more accurately what is really concerning him. Furthermore, when the sender of a message receives feedback—hears what impression another is getting—it helps that person reflect more deeply about what he has just said. Usually this prompts a fuller disclosure of the problem. And once you really understand what's going on, you can start to solve the problems or address the issues. For example, in this situation the buyer might now say "You bet I am. Your late deliveries are causing me big problems on my production line."

Active listening is a challenging skill to learn. It requires true concentration on what the other person is saying. Many times this means listening to more than what is being said and being sensitive to the nonverbals in the message also. In addition, this skill involves addressing the feeling or emotions in the message. For many people, this is uncomfortable, and yet that is where the true power of active listening lies.

Active listening is a very powerful tool to use in building synergistic relationships. By using an active listening response, you not only clarify the information you heard to make sure you're on the same wavelength with the buyer, but also you prove that you understood his message. He feels good that his communication was heard. In addition, active listening requires that you listen more intently, providing you the opportunity to be more accurate in your understanding of his message.

There are other benefits. Since active listening does not convey judgment or evaluation of the other person, she feels your acceptance—she feels safer and is more likely to trust you. This allows her to get the real feelings, or the true issues, out. Active listening shows your willingness to listen and your concern for her needs; as a result, she'll be more likely to give you equal time and listen to you. In addition, your active-listening skill allows you to hear "what's not being said" for a richer understanding of the other person. You'll actually be able to grasp the meaning of a message deeper than the spoken words.

Active listening can be misused, though, creating frustration for both of you. Here are some guidelines to make sure active listening works for you. The most effective use of active listening is when

1. the other person is clearly upset or concerned;
2. you get an indication that the other person wants to talk about the concern with you;

3. you genuinely feel accepting of the other person and the problem being expressed; you don't have to like the problem or take pleasure in hearing about it, just feel okay about listening to it;
4. the time and place seem right; don't start listening to a serious concern with only five minutes to spare, for example.

Do not employ active listening when

1. any of the above conditions are not present, especially the first one; active listening can be irritating, as well as time-consuming, if you do it all the time—what's more, incessant use of this response can lead the other person to feel that you are using a technique on them rather than being yourself;
2. the other person truly needs facts, information, or other forms of concrete assistance from you; when someone asks you where the bathroom is, don't respond with, "Sounds like you're feeling a lot of pressure in your lower abdomen!" Likewise, when buyers request information about your product, price, company, and the like, just give them the information they need to make a buying decision.

HABITS TO DEVELOP

First off, don't start every active listening response the same way. It not only can become monotonous; it also can create the impression that you are just using a mechanical technique, not showing genuine concern. Here are some phrases you can use when you feel quite certain you understand what has been said:

"You feel . . ."
"What I hear you saying . . ."
"From your point of view . . ."

"It seems to you . . ."
"From where you stand . . ."
"I'm picking up that you . . ."
"As you see it . . ."
"I really hear you saying that . . ."
"Where you're coming from . . ."

When you feel tentative and less certain you understand, you want to express this as well:

"I think I hear you saying . . ."
"I wonder if . . ."
"It appears you . . ."
"I'm not sure I'm with you, but . . ."
"Correct me if I'm wrong, but . . ."
"Is it possible that . . ."
"Let me see if I understand; you . . ."

Second, every statement does not require an active listening response. Sometimes you need to use the passive listening skills: silence, acknowledgments, and door openers. For example, when the other person has sent a very clear expression of her feelings, an acknowledgment of "uh-huh" may be more appropriate than a near word-for-word repetition.

Mastering the skill of active listening means dropping one's own agenda and understanding the world from another's viewpoint. Carl Rogers, in his book *A Way of Being*, has this definition for the active listener's "way of being":

An empathic way of being with another person has several facets. It means entering the private perceptual world of the other and becoming thoroughly at home with it. It involves being sensitive, moment by moment, to the changing felt meanings which flow in this other person, to the fear or rage or tenderness or confusion or whatever that he or she is experiencing. It means temporarily living in the other's life, moving about in it delicately without making judge-ments; it means sensing meanings of which he or she is scarcely aware, but not trying to uncover totally unconscious feelings, since this would be too threatening. It includes communicating your sensings of the person's world as you look with fresh and unfrightened eyes at elements of which he or she is fearful. It means frequently checking with the other person as to the accuracy of your sensings, and being guided by the responses you receive. You are a confident companion to the person in his or her inner world.

The biggest obstacle to listening at this level is your own beliefs and filters. In the diagram of the communication process used to explain active listening, the boxes are marked *Encoding* and *Decoding*. They graphically represent our filter system, our paradigms. As we listen to others, our filters can distort the original message.

Take this example from a medical supply company. The doctor whom the salesperson was calling on simply said, "Jane, could you come back next week? I've got surgery in an hour and I'm running late."

This was simple and direct enough, but Jane heard something different. Her experience had been that doctors have big egos and that they never give salespeople enough of their time. So she heard his message as putting her off—as saying that she wasn't important. Whether the doctor meant to communicate this or not doesn't matter, because Jane left vowing she would push even harder in the future. A message she was making up was causing her stress and perhaps even jeopardizing the relationship.

Here is another example that illustrates what happens when our agendas get in the way.

A participant in one of our workshops, Paul, shared a problem that was creating a great deal of concern and frustration for him at work. He was the supervisor of the field software engineers for his computer graphics company. His people were responsible for getting their clients operational whenever they had a software breakdown. Naturally, time was important and his field people all carried beepers. It so happened that the beeper bill was not paid, and they were not functional when a major client's computer system went down. The client couldn't contact the field engineer who handled the account, and the time delay caused a real problem for them.

To demonstrate the active listening skills, the facilitator (the workshop leader) queried him as follows:

PAUL: Well, I was so upset that I decided to take it upon myself to call New York [the home office] and find out what happened and why the invoice wasn't paid.

FACILITATOR: You were pretty exasperated by then.

PAUL: You bet I was. But that was nothing compared to what I found out next.

FACILITATOR: Go ahead. (nodding)

PAUL: Well, I was told that we were in a major cash bind and that all invoices were set up for a 120-day payment cycle. And that my problem was the least of their worries.

FACILITATOR: You're kidding! Why didn't they tell you, so you could tell your vendors what to expect?

PAUL: I don't know.

FACILITATOR: Well, is this true for all vendors?

PAUL: That's what I was told.

FACILITATOR: Well, who made this decision?

By this time a couple of people in the class began chuckling, and the role play was stopped to assess what had happened. It was then that the facilitator noticed his whole demeanor had changed; Paul had noticed the change also. All of a sudden he felt the conversation had pulled away from him and his problem. The facilitator realized what had happened and shared it with the group. When Paul said that all invoices were put on a 120-day payment cycle, the facilitator saw our invoice (and his paycheck) sitting on someone's desk and he got upset. He was no longer able to listen to Paul's problem because of his own agenda.

This is the point that makes the paradigm shift in sales so

critical. If you are living in the traditional, adversarial model of controlling and leading the conversation, you will always in your head be developing strategy and the necessary tactics to close the sale. Only when you recognize that the most important goal is to understand the buyer, and her unique perception of her world, will you be able to master listening. Truthfully, it is only then that you know how your products and services will fit the buyer's needs.

Active listening provides the opportunity for individuals to feel heard and understood. As a result, they feel comfortable discussing the situation, and eventually the real issue surfaces. Here's an example of truly listening and understanding the views of a buyer in a sales situation where most of us would get a little defensive.

BUYER: Jim, thanks for coming over. I've got to tell you that I am really upset with you and your customer-support people. This place is going crazy, and everyone is yelling at me about the problems with your system.

SELLER: Bob, I'm sorry for what you're going through. It sounds like the installation has created some headaches for you and your people.

BUYER: It sure has and we can't get any response from your support people. They don't seem to care about our ongoing operation.

SELLER: So you don't feel they're being sensitive to your needs. Bob, would you fill me in a little?

BUYER: They're *not* sensitive to our needs. Yesterday we got flooded with new orders to enter into the system, and then we started getting revisions to orders before they were even in the system. Talk about a paperwork nightmare. Our people were convinced that something was wrong with the system, since it seemed to be running slow. When Sam called your people to have someone check it out, they said it would be today before they could send someone over. Sam got upset and climbed all over my boss, and you can imagine what he said to me. He's had doubts about this system all along, and every time a situation like yesterday comes up, he uses it as evidence to support his case.

SELLER: No wonder you're concerned; you stuck your neck out to buy the new system, and when there's a problem you feel like your job credibility is on the line.

BUYER: That's right, Jim, and what are you going to do to get your customer-support people to do what they are supposed to?

SELLER: Sounds like you are looking to us for the answers, so here is what I see as the issues we need to look at. First of all, I'm hearing that some more training might be in order. The original problem flared up when Sam's people ran into a heavier-than-normal volume, and assuming for a moment the system is running okay, we should look at what happened. Second, I heard your concern over our response time. I think we should get Sam and our people together again to clearly define your needs, and ours, to establish guidelines acceptable to both. And third is the concern of your boss. We obviously have not gotten his total buy-in and support. I would also like to address his issues and get him on our team. That will save you a lot of stress in the future. Does that sound like a reasonable way to look at the situation?

BUYER: You bet. Let's get started right now.

In this situation, any defensive response would have stifled the flow of communications and prevented Jim and Bob from getting to the core issues. Imagine how different this conversation would have been if Jim had responded to Bob's initial comment with one of these typical sales responses:

BUYER: Jim, thanks for coming over. I've got to tell you that I am really upset with you and your customer-support people. This place is going crazy, and everyone is yelling at me about the problems with your system.

SELLER: Well, Bob, I'm not surprised. I told you that we needed more training time with your people.

Or:

BUYER: Jim, thanks for coming over. I've got to tell you that I am really upset with you and your customer-support people. This place is going crazy, and everyone is yelling at me about the problems with your system.
SELLER: Don't worry about it, Bob. Tell me what's going on, and I'll take care of it pronto.

Or:

BUYER: Jim, thanks for coming over. I've got to tell you that I am really upset with you and your customer-support people. This place is going crazy, and everyone is yelling at me about the problems with your system.
SELLER: Bob. I'm really sorry for the problem. You're the third complaint I've had today. I don't understand what's going on with our people.

In our original scenario, all four of the seller responses utilize active listening to ensure that Bob knows he's been heard and understood. In the final response, Jim even takes a moment to summarize the entire conversation to make sure they are on the same wavelength. Then he begins to offer some solutions.

As a result, Jim clarified the information and demonstrated to Bob that he was concerned and understood the implications of Bob's problem. Moreover, they were able to get all the issues out on the table, including the critical issue of Bob's problem with his boss.

Typically, the problem that is expressed at first is not the central issue, and the listener must suspend judgments, evaluations, and solutions until the speaker has had an opportunity to vent all feelings and has gotten all issues out on the table. Notice in this example that the conversation begins with the operating problem with the new system, goes then to the lack of response from the customer-support people, and moves finally to Bob's concern over his credibility with his boss. This is certainly the core issue for him. This deeper level of self-disclosure occurs when the speaker feels you have come over to their side and understood the situation from their point of view. Then, and only then, can collaborative problem solving begin. None of this occurs in the situations where traditional sales responses are used.

By identifying and defining the three levels of listening, you will be better able to grasp the importance of continually developing your skills. Recognize that listening is a necessary skill in the new paradigm. Mastering the skill of listening will dramatically improve not only your success in selling but also the joy and satisfaction you get from relating more effectively to others in your life.

Chapter Summary

1. Listening is an essential tool for building synergistic relationships with others.
2. The four major reasons why we don't listen effectively are
   - we didn't learn how to listen;
   - we believe that selling is talking;
   - listening requires focused concentration;
   - our paradigms distort what we hear.
3. The three skills of an effective listener are
   - attending behaviors—nonverbal listening;
   - passive listening—including silence, acknowledgment, and door openers;
   - active listening—paraphrasing back your perception of the message.
4. Active listening is sending back a message that includes your understanding of the facts and feelings in the sender's message.
5. Active listening is a very powerful tool in building relationships with others as it lets the other person know you have heard and understood their communication.

CHAPTER FIVE

GREATER SALES RESULTS

THROUGH LISTENING

I don't care how much you know until I know how much you care.

—*ANONYMOUS ZEN MASTER*

In the first chapter, we told the story about the airline that lost the $4 million a year account when senior management took a stronger position in renegotiating the contract with the client. As a result, the client signed with another carrier for the next year. During that year, John, a sales manager with a natural propensity for listening to his clients and a graduate of the Synergistic Selling course where he had sharpened his skills, was transferred to the district that included this client.

He established contact with the client and listened to the complaints from the key people. As he says, he allowed them to "bare their souls." During the conversation, the clients accused John's company of many things, some of which weren't true; but John just listened. He did not get defensive or throw any blame their way. Nor did he call them on some things they had said and done during the relationship. As a result of the open and uninterrupted flow of communication, John allowed the clients to get rid of their emotions and purge their anxiety. They felt that he truly understood their point of view. Once this was done, he was able to negotiate a new agreement and save the relationship—and $4 million in revenue.

Listening fully to another person sets the stage for what you say in reply. Not only does it provide you the opportunity to learn about the other person and their world, but also it demonstrates your willingness to understand and accept their viewpoint. This provides a role model for the relationship, and usually you'll find the other person more willing to understand and accept your view in turn. On the flip side, when a person doesn't feel heard and understood, she becomes more focused on getting her point across, defending her position, or withdrawing because she doesn't feel that you care. As a result, she is not able to, or does not care to, hear you out.

If you don't first listen to the needs and concerns of the other person, your ideas, solutions to her problems, or information on your products and services will fall on deaf ears. In selling, the difference between a know-it-all and a source of knowledge depends on when you share your knowledge. The buyer doesn't care how much you know until she knows how much you care.

There are three primary times in the seller-buyer relationship when effective listening skills are essential: when the buyer voices unmet needs and fears, when the buyer voices resistance to change, and when the buyer voices complaints and/or other problems.

LISTENING FOR THE BUYER'S UNMET NEEDS AND FEARS

This step is the basis for the rest of the process and can make or break the relationship. At the beginning, buyers address the factors that will influence their buying decision. Many of these factors are influenced by their own paradigms, or belief systems, that relate to their decision, many of which are subconscious. As a result, buyers may appear to operate on automatic pilot—almost in a rut. Their paradigms define the boundaries of their decisions, and they will accept only what is acceptable within those boundaries.

In the traditional model of sales, the salesperson probes for the buyer's needs. He asks questions to uncover information that he then uses as ammunition for his presentation. In other words, the probing process is used to uncover information needed to "load the presentation." From this context, it is impossible to ask questions that do not come across to the buyer as "probes" that meet the salesperson's needs to lead the buyer to a predetermined outcome—buying the salesperson's product or service. If a buyer feels led, controlled, or manipulated through this process, she tends to shut down and otherwise resist the salesperson.

In Step 1 of the buyer's decision-making process in the Synergistic Paradigm, the salesperson encourages the buyer to talk, then listens to understand her views and unique needs and fears relating to her decision. This means listening without an agenda or predetermined outcome. Only in this manner can a salesperson fulfill the consultant role in the relationship.

This process will occur only when a salesperson genuinely listens to a buyer without imposing his agenda. Participants in our seminars are surprised when they discover how different the salesperson's role can be once they have listened to a buyer and demonstrated how much they care. This means listening to understand and accept the buyer's position. Typically, salespeople get blocked by their need to listen for buying clues, to probe for appropriate information, or to find ammunition for their presentation.

True, the salesperson brings expertise and experience to the relationship, but it's of no value unless the buyer has expressed a need for it. Only after thoroughly understanding the buyer's needs or problems can a salesperson determine whether or not his product or service is the best solution for the buyer.

In addition to bringing new expertise and quality products or services, the professional salesperson provides additional benefits to the partnership with the buyer. One important benefit is that the salesperson provides a different set of eyes—a fresh look that can enable the buyer to make a more effective decision.

The salesperson also provides an opportunity for a buyer to understand and focus on her goals, thus helping her see her options with greater clarity. This results in more effective and more satisfying decisions for the buyer.

Finally, the salesperson provides the stimulation for a buyer to think through the factors that will influence her final decision. Today's challenging and complex business environment requires new solutions to age-old problems. Your buyers will have a tendency to fall back on the same solutions (the same decisions) they have always used, but still expect different results. A salesperson may, in fact, be the one in the relationship who influences the other to see differently, thus facilitating a paradigm shift.

Here are some pitfalls to avoid while listening during Step 1 of the buyer's decision-making process.

YOU CONTROL THE CONVERSATION THROUGH
LEADING QUESTIONS

This means asking questions in a way that solicits a specific answer or leads the buyer in a specific direction. Here are some examples a salesperson representing a travel agency might use with the travel manager of a major corporation.

"Would you find it useful to have month-end reports showing all of the travel expenses by individual or department?" The salesperson asking this question is looking for a yes answer, and the buyer knows it because it's obviously a benefit the agency provides. As a result, she'll feel led and manipulated. The real message behind this question is "We provide month-end travel reports by individual or department for a more accurate analysis of your travel expenditures." So just say it that way.

"Don't you agree that our 800 number would provide an extra service to your people when they have a problem out-of-town?" Again, the salesperson is looking for agreement, a yes answer. Traditional sales training teaches the importance of getting agreement. This is not true if the buyer feels you are controlling the conversation. The buyer doesn't necessarily want to agree with you, he wants you to understand his viewpoint.

"How do you think your boss would feel about our new lowest-rate-possible guarantee program?" It's obvious, isn't it? The buyer is feeling led, manipulated, and probably even put down by such elementary questions. Yet they occur with great frequency in sales calls where the salesperson feels a need to control the flow of conversation.

YOU FORCE BUYERS TO DEFEND THEIR POSITION
BY ASKING "WHY" QUESTIONS

Many times when people are asked to defend their position or their beliefs, they actually become more entrenched in their position. As a result, they become less open to looking at other alternatives. For example, the buyer says, "Well, actually I prefer to use a smaller agency."

Notice the difference between the seller's response #1 and response #2.

Response #1: "Why do you feel a smaller agency is better?"

Response #2: "So as far as you're concerned, a smaller agency is better."

In the first case the seller and buyer are on opposite sides of the desk with the buyer defending his position, and in the second, the seller has come over to the buyer's side to gain a better understanding of the buyer's beliefs. Response #1 forces the buyer to justify his statements as if they were wrong, and response #2 communicates acceptance and understanding that will encourage more communication on the subject. The buyer might respond to #1 with "Because I get better service" and to #2 with "Yeah, it seems like I get better service." Even if you get the same information, there are subtle yet major impacts on the relationship.

In most cases, however, the second response (an example of active listening) will encourage the buyer to talk more. For example, the buyer might respond, "Yeah, it seems like I get better service. For example, three of the women at our agency actually recognize my voice when I call." So we've also discovered another point that is important to our buyer.

Here's another example. The buyer says: "I just think you guys are too far away. I need an agency that's close by."

Response #1: "Why do you think we're too far away, especially since we do provide ticket delivery?"

Response #2: "So the fact that our office is farther away creates a problem for you."

Again, notice the difference in the two responses and remember the salesperson's objective in Step 1 is to gain a thorough understanding of the buyer's viewpoint.

YOU JUDGE AND EVALUATE WHAT THE BUYER SAYS

By doing this, the salesperson is creating a debating environment rather than one of collaboration. Once the salesperson starts agreeing or disagreeing, the buyer will follow suit when the salesperson speaks. It is vital to realize that the goal of Step 1 is simply to understand the buyer's view without your own judgments of what should be done.

To use the first example above, the buyer says, "Well, actually I prefer to use a smaller agency."

A judgmental response would be, "But a smaller agency can't provide you the same consistent level of service that we can." That response says, "You're wrong for thinking what you think," which reinforces the typical adversarial nature of the seller-buyer relationship.

In the second example, the buyer says, "I just think you guys are too far away. I need an agency that's close by." Examples of responses that judge and evaluate what the buyer is saying would be, "Well, it's really not that far" or "That really shouldn't be a problem since we deliver tickets."

Again, those responses simply keep the chess game between the seller and buyer going. There's no willingness just to get the buyer's message and understand it.

YOU HEAR "BUYING SIGNALS" AND JUMP INTO THE SELLING MODE

The natural tendency for most salespeople is to begin selling when they hear a buyer state a need that they can meet. They quit listening and start selling. This limits the flow of the conversation and teaches buyers to stop sharing their needs so that the salesperson will quit selling.

A "buying signal" in our travel agency example might be, "One of the things that is really important is the quality of the month-end reports. With today's rising travel costs, it's important to keep track of the expenses."

Most salespeople immediately discuss how great their month-end reports are and how happy their other clients are. However, the goal again is to simply understand what the buyer is saying and acknowledge its validity.

That might sound like, "So the availability and accuracy of the month-end reports are important to you. What other factors do you look at when selecting your travel firm?" The response that listens to and understands the buyer is much more effective than the typical Ping-Pong match of "You give me a need and I'll tell you how we do that," and then "Give me another need, and I'll tell you how good we are at that."

As a result of listening at Step 1, the buyer is encouraged to open up to you. You are building a strong foundation for a partnership, one based on open and honest communication, not control and manipulation. Let the buyer get his needs off his chest first.

Following is a script of a portion of a sales call in Step 1, *identifying and defining unmet needs and fears.* This script incorporates the listening skills covered in chapter 4. Pay particular attention to two things:

1. the type of questions asked; notice the role of the facilitator, how open-ended questions are used rather than probes, especially those that encourage the buyer to look deeper at those issues facing her;
2. the active listening responses and how they let the buyer know that the salesperson has understood and accepted what she has said (you may wish to review the information on active listening in chapter 4).

The example takes place in the buyer's office. He is the new vice president of sales and marketing for the organization, and the salesperson represents a sales-training company. We pick up the conversation in progress.

SELLER (1): In other words, from what you've seen in the six months you've been here, your objective this first year is to get your people more proactive in the marketplace and more skillful in closing business.

BUYER: That's right. This was supported by the recent survey we conducted. We asked our customers, past and present, to evaluate our salespeople, and they responded that our people needed to be more professional in their sales approach. The general picture is that our salespeople come across as order-takers and they are not seen by our buyers as being effective in their jobs.

SELLER (2): So even your buyers are looking for something else out of your people.

BUYER: Yeah, and my guess is that they want them more involved in the overall sales process. Ours is a complicated business, and our customers want someone who does more than write the order. They want a knowledgeable person who will get things done inside our organization also.

SELLER (3): You sound pretty convinced this isn't happening right now.

BUYER: You bet. That survey simply reinforced what I have seen since I got here. But I'm not sure training is the answer.

SELLER (4): Sounds like you have some concerns over what training could do for you.

BUYER: Well, that's part of it. I just left an organization that spent a fortune on sales training, and I'm not sure I could see any results. But what I meant was that there is an overall apathy in the atmosphere here that I don't think training could do anything about. It seems to be built into the culture. You know the attitude. We've been successful this way for years, why change it? ... That's interesting, I've never spoken that out loud.

SELLER (5): Let's focus on the culture issue for a moment since it seems that one has some deeper implications for you. What are the key areas critical to that culture that you see need changing?

BUYER: Well, there are two that I've noticed. One is that because of the complexity of our business, which I mentioned before, we have a lot of rules and regulations created by our operations and manufacturing people through the years that make it difficult for our customers and salespeople. So I don't feel that we are very customer focused in other areas of the company. And second, the executive committee doesn't really talk about these deeper issues. George, the president, is really direct in his approach and seems to intimidate people. He is well liked, but people here don't really speak the truth. It's like everybody gets along on the surface, but there's a lot of other stuff going on behind the scenes.

SELLER (6): What's the possibility of this situation changing?

BUYER: Not much. It seems pretty well entrenched, and no one wants to be the one to speak up. However ... (silence)

SELLER (7): You're hesitating.

BUYER: Yeah, I was just thinking that that may be the reason they brought me in from the outside. That even came up in the interview with George. If so, I better take another look at things before I get adjusted to the status quo and lose my ability to see with a different set of eyes. So I'll tell you what. Let's focus on the sales training, and I'll look at the culture change issues. Maybe we can do something that fits together.

SELLER (8): Okay, great. But first, I would like to hear more about your issues with training as a result of your last job. It sounds to me like you were really disappointed in the results.

Most salespeople would have stayed focused on the sales-training issue and asked a series of questions to find out how many salespeople there were, what training they've received, and so on. That's what is important to the salesperson for her presentation. As a result, she would have missed the opportunity to discover some underlying issues for the buyer, ones that help the salesperson understand the total picture from the buyer's perspective. Only by letting go of her agenda and listening without directing the buyer can this occur.

Let's look at each response and how she handled the situation. In #1 and #2, the salesperson summarizes the conversation by feeding back the information she heard. Responses #3 and #4 are excellent examples of active listening. And #5 and #6 are open-ended questions. Notice that the questions are not slanted in any way to solicit a specific answer or lead the buyer in a predetermined direction. In response #7, the seller actually active-listens the silence in the previous message, and #8 is another active-listening response.

Notice how smooth the conversation is when the salesperson gets out of the way and simply listens to understand her buyer's situation.

LISTENING TO THE BUYER'S RESISTANCE
TO CHANGE

Another application of listening skills is responding to the buyer's resistance to change. In the traditional model, this is called "overcoming objections." In other words, the buyer has thrown you an obstacle to overcome in your strategy to close the sale. For example, if the buyer says, I'm not sure your product will impact our operation that much," the typical salesperson's reaction is to immediately show the buyer the research and data that prove it will. It's as if your opponent on the chess table has made a surprise move and you must develop a strategy to overcome it. As we have stressed before, that adversarial approach will get you nowhere. Instead, look at the message as a communication from your partner asking for help.

In chapter 3 we quoted psychologist Kurt Lewin and his work on the change process. Lewin's work showed that for people to change their beliefs they must have an opportunity to express their allegiance and loyalty to their old beliefs and their fear and doubt about changing their beliefs.

The selling-buying process generally leads to change, and so naturally buyers will express loyalty to the old and fear and doubt about the new. It's nothing to get excited about. But what happens is the salesperson gets worried, considers the comment an objection, and proceeds to prove the buyer wrong. The buyer then defends her beliefs and, in many cases, becomes more entrenched in those beliefs. The salesperson introduces even more data to prove the buyer wrong, and she again defends her position, becoming even more resistant. The more the salesperson pushes, the more the buyer resists.

Co-author Tom Gordon addressed this issue in an article published in 1960 in *Guideposts and Methods,* a publication of National Sales Executives, Inc. In that article he wrote:

In recent years, psychology, as a science, has had a kind of break-through, and I am rather enthusiastically convinced that some of the things that have been going on as a result of this break-through have relevance, significance and promise for the field of selling.

Like break-throughs in other sciences, the one in psychology has not resulted from a single discovery, but rather from the findings of many different and unrelated studies. These findings have contributed to the emergence of a new way of looking at human behavior, particularly how human behavior gets changed or how people are influenced to change.

I am assuming that the selling process itself is often a change process—a process in which a prospective customer has to make certain changes in their attitudes or opinions, if they are to buy the product or services which the salesperson offers.

He went on to provide research from psychological studies dealing with change. These particular studies were undertaken for the purpose of investigating the process by which psychological counselors facilitate changes in the attitudes and behavior of their clients. Because psychological counseling is essentially a process involving face-to-face communication between two people, these studies naturally focused on analyzing the verbal communication of the counselor and client.

One of the most interesting findings from these studies, and the one having possible application to the selling process, had to do with the counselor's communication and its effect on the client. The investigators discovered that some counselors stood out from others with regard to the following: (1) they talked less and listened more; (2) they made few or no suggestions; (3) they gave little or no advice and avoided evaluating or judging the client or their ideas; (4) they used no persuasion, arguments, logic, selling; (5) they let the client direct the interview themselves, decide what to talk about; and (6) they left responsibility with the client with respect to decisions about their life and avoided influencing them to make a particular decision.

Surprisingly enough, the clients of such counselors responded to this "nondirective" approach in the following ways: (1) they showed little or no resistance or defensiveness—there was nothing for them to push against or argue with; (2) they talked more, expressed deeper and deeper feelings, got to their "truer" feelings quicker; (3) as they began to believe the counselor was not going to do anything to them, they began to feel safe, unpushed, unmanipulated, in charge of themselves; (4) as they began to feel the counselor really understood their point of view, they felt freer to share with them things they had never expressed to anyone else; and (5) finally, they began to change their feelings, attitudes, and behavior themselves—self-directed change, change freely chosen—they were doing the changing, not being influenced or pressured to change.

What we are saying, then, is that if the salesperson listens to the buyer, he is providing a safe space for the buyer to address all of the issues regarding their decision and the change it represents. If the feelings about the process of change—and they are always there—aren't expressed, they lie below the surface and block the flow of the process. To facilitate the change process means providing the opportunity for the buyer to openly express their allegiance to the old attitudes and behaviors and their fear and doubts about the new. This is what Lewin meant by "unfreezing the present belief system."

Salespeople can facilitate this change process effectively if they remember these points:

1. Understand, and accept the buyer's feelings about the change process through the use of active listening. You may believe that you have understood the message, but the other person isn't sure of that until you have demonstrated your understanding by repeating the message back in your own words.
2. Avoid the fix-it mentality. In many cases, the mere fact that buyers have communicated their concerns will resolve the issue for them. If not, the salesperson

may need to provide additional information to help
the buyer resolve the issue for himself. A salesperson
enhances her effectiveness in facilitating the change
process if she remembers her role is not to
overcome the *resistance to change*, but to provide the
value that fuels the other person's *motivation to change*.
3. The initial concern that the buyer expresses may
not be the core issue. Most people don't take the
time to look at the core issues underlying their concerns
about change. A good listener provides the climate
for people to talk it out and in the process discover
the more basic issues. Once they are identified, both
seller and buyer can work together to resolve these
concerns.

The following examples illustrate the value of these three
points. In the first situation, the salesperson responds to the
buyer's resistance to change in a pretty typical fashion:

BUYER: Jim, our people really enjoy the sales-training program we've been using, and our managers like the fact
that their salespeople are only out of the field for one day.
SELLER: Okay, Nancy, I hear what you're saying, but our research shows that it takes at least three days of training
in the classroom for salespeople to learn and use these
skills. And anyway, your managers would really be happier if their people were better-trained and closed more
business. Right? How you get them there shouldn't be
their concern.
BUYER: Even if I did agree with you, Jim, there's no way I
could get that change through right now. I'm not sure my
boss is open to any changes in the courses we offer.
SELLER: Well, how about this as an option? We could schedule
a special pilot program at a reduced rate and have the
participants compare the two courses. That could provide
us some first-hand feedback to help you sell the course internally.

BUYER: No, I can't do that. We don't have any money in the budget for pilot programs right now.

SELLER: Then how about scheduling a presentation one morning? You get the right people together, and I'll give them an overview of the course.

BUYER: Jim, that's really not possible right now. We are swamped with everything else going on around here. But thanks anyway. I'll keep that offer in mind for the future.

As you can see, Jim counters every one of Nancy's concerns, and she counters by resisting.

This does not communicate understanding and acceptance. No listening equals no progress. Notice also Jim's first response. In our training courses we hear participants saying, "I hear what you're saying, but ..." or "I understand your concerns, but ..." and think they've demonstrated understanding. They haven't. First of all, simply saying you understand isn't as powerful as demonstrating it by restating your interpretation of their message. And second, the "but" discounts the first part of the message, "I understand" or "I hear." "But" really says: the following information will prove you wrong.

Let's present the same situation using effective listening skills and remembering the points reviewed earlier.

BUYER: Jim, our people really enjoy the sales-training program we've been using, and our managers like the fact that their salespeople are only out of the field for one day.

SELLER: So you're comfortable with the way things are going right now.

BUYER: No, I'm not totally comfortable with it, but my customers, the field salespeople, and their managers are. Personally, I don't feel the program really has the impact I think it should.

SELLER: What's missing for you?

BUYER: Well, two things for sure. First of all, one day simply isn't sufficient to provide the salespeople the skills they need, and second, there's no follow-up when they get back to the field. So the one day really doesn't accomplish much.

SELLER: Sounds to me like there's a difference between your expectations and the field's.

BUYER: Yeah, and I'm not sure what to do about it. I mean everything's going okay as far as they're concerned. It's just that I see so much more possibility. With everything else going on around here, I'm not sure they'll consider any changes.

SELLER: You're apprehensive about recommending changes.

BUYER: Yeah, I guess so, and I've been thinking about that a lot lately.

SELLER: About making changes here?

BUYER: Yeah, I've seen that I've been hesitant to really push for some of the changes I think we need to make and how that doesn't work for me. I've seen from this conversation it really is time to make some of my recommendations known. So let me give that some more thought. Call me next week and we'll get together. Once I've determined the changes I want to make, I want to talk with you about how your training might fit in.

In the second situation, the salesperson's listening allowed the conversation to flow into a totally different direction. Not where the seller thought it should go, but to the problems the buyer is actually experiencing. Because the seller shows he understands the buyer's world, he has begun building a partnership. He has facilitated the buyer's initial resistance to change rather than trying to resolve or "fix" the buyer's concerns. Notice also how the seller's listening provided the climate that allowed the buyer to get past the surface of the sales-training problem and address some core issues.

This is an example of the totally new level of communication and relationship that can be created with effective listening skills which ultimately facilitate the change process.

LISTENING TO THE BUYER'S COMPLAINTS
AND/OR OTHER PROBLEMS

Needless to say, salespeople prefer happy customers; it's not only more pleasant and enjoyable to work with people who are positive, enthusiastic, and contented; it's also conducive to productive sales calls. Customers who are upset, worried, or angry simply cannot focus their attention on your product or service. So it's generally in the interest of the partnership for the salesperson to attempt to aid, counsel, or otherwise offer some form of relief. Not much progress will take place during a sales call until the customer sufficiently resolves her troubles.

This situation may occur in the middle of a sales call—for a variety of reasons—or may be present when the salesperson first arrives. What's important is to recognize the clues that the customer is upset and to take the appropriate action. One obvious clue that the customer is upset is a clear statement to that effect. Comments like "I should have stayed in bed this morning," "Everything that could go wrong has gone wrong," and "I've got a bone to pick with you" tell even the most inattentive listener that something is wrong. More often, however, the clues are more subtle, even unspoken. The buyer may look upset or sound upset through voice tone, facial expressions, or posture; the buyer seems to be avoiding you or has gradually reduced his volume of business with you.

Salespeople need to sharpen their senses and pay close attention to these signals of trouble so that they can offer an understanding ear at the earliest possible time. This is especially important in the case of the customer who is showing signs of discontent with the salesperson or her products or services. If the early warning signs are missed or ignored, it may be too late once the customer's dissatisfaction has come out in the open.

When it comes to helping another person who is feeling upset or troubled, some people just seem to have a gift for listening and responding fully. For most of us, this gift is limited or doesn't exist at all. This is where skillful application of effective listening skills is of invaluable assistance.

Unfortunately, this is not the natural tendency for most people; all too often, they take approaches to helping that prove unhelpful, even if they do want to be positive and caring. These unhelpful approaches are best called "communication roadblocks" because they so often do just that—throw up a barrier in front of the troubled person, thus discouraging further communication.

Certainly these roadblock responses don't cause a problem every time and with every person. However, they always run a fairly high risk of proving unhelpful to the relationship. The following is a description of the eight major types of roadblocks. There are, of course, endless variations, but the examples shown here are typical.

All of the sample dialogue is based on the following scene: a salesperson is making a first call on a customer who had previously been serviced by this salesperson's predecessor. As it turns out, the customer had a very poor experience with the earlier salesperson: late deliveries, missed appointments, order mix-ups, and so on. This all comes out in a long tirade against the former salesperson, the company, and its products.

ROADBLOCK GROUP 1: DENYING, MINIMIZING, DISTRACTING

"Oh, it can't be as bad as all that."
"I'm sure there's just been a little misunderstanding somewhere."
"Well, that's the past. Let's get our relationship started right."

All of these responses may be intended to help, but they actually avoid facing the problem. The salesperson doesn't want the customer to be upset, so he tries to sweep it under the rug. This can result in the customer's feeling unheard. Chances are she will react by feeling irritated, frustrated, and unwilling to share more of the problem.

ROADBLOCK GROUP 2: CHEERING UP, REASSURING,
ENCOURAGING

"I'm sure nothing like that will happen again."
*"Well, look at the bright side. Now we know what
problems to start on."*
*"Don't worry about it anymore. I promise you it won't
happen again."*

In contrast to popular thinking, attempts to cheer up some-body usually fail miserably. People who are upset mainly want to feel heard out. They also need to unload their feelings—to get them out of their system. This group of roadblocks tends to discount the other's feelings and suggests that they be set aside and forgotten. A troubled customer will likely both re-ject them and feel put off by them.

ROADBLOCK GROUP 3: SYMPATHETIC INDIGNATION, ME TOOING,
STORY TELLING

"Gee, that's too bad."
"That happened to me once. It was two years ago and . . ."
*"You shouldn't have had to put up with that. Our company
should have straightened it out earlier."*

Almost no one is turned off by a sincere and warm expression of sympathy like "I'm sorry to hear that." But when the lis-tener steals the spotlight and begins telling "war stories" to prove they can identify with the problem, the listener can feel left out. The troubled person doesn't have a chance to con-tinue expressing herself; rather, the tables are now so turned that the upset person has to listen.

Another problem with either insincere or overdone sym-pathy is that the upset person often is made to feel inferior or inadequate. This can lead to irritation and indignation: "I don't need your pity."

ROADBLOCK GROUP 4: ADVISING, TEACHING, DIRECTING

"Now, what I would do about that is ..."
"You should have called Nancy Smith at the regional
office."
"If you ever have delivery problems again, call this
number."

Giving advice is probably the most popular form of "helping" and the most abused. Although many people do want advice and actively seek it out, just as many don't, especially when it is uninvited. And even when advice is asked for, it is often judgmental and critical; this leaves the upset person feeling more frustrated. Finally, giving specific directions runs the risk of alienating the other person, making them feel as though they're incompetent to handle things on their own.

ROADBLOCK GROUP 5: TAKING OVER, RESCUING,
MARTYRING

"Let me call and see if I can get you a rebate for the
problems you went through."
"We should have done a better job of staying on top
of the situation. How can I make it up to you?"
"I'll take care of those problems. Don't give 'em another
thought."

Contrary to popular thinking, people often don't like being rescued. They can feel helpless, embarrassed, or resentful toward the uninvited do-gooder. A salesperson often wants to take control of his customer's problems for fear they will block the sale if not quickly resolved. This attitude can lead not only to customer resentment but also to actual dollar-and-cent losses to the salesperson who offered to handle the problem or make unnecessary restitution.

The salesperson's job is not to take on the problem, but to provide, when possible, acceptable ways to solve it.

ROADBLOCK GROUP 6: ANALYZING, PROBING, PLAYING DETECTIVE

"That probably happened to you because . . ."
"When, why, where, who, what?"
"What happened when you complained?"

Too often analysis or questioning comes across as interrogation, invasion of privacy, or veiled criticism, especially "why" questions. This group of roadblocks is similar to Group 5 in that both communicate the attitude that the customer really cannot handle the problem and should turn it over to the salesperson.

ROADBLOCK GROUP 7: CRITICIZING, MORALIZING, WARNING

"You probably brought that on by being too lenient
to begin with."
"You just can't count on anyone today."
"Listen, if you have problems like that with me, you
have to tell me to my face."

In many cases, the listener who uses this type of roadblock is actually feeling critical of the upset person, and as a result she communicates her feelings back, thus eliminating any opportunity to resolve the issue. Use of this roadblock group demonstrates vividly that your judgments have gotten in the way of your ability to listen.

ROADBLOCK GROUP 8: ARGUING, DEFENDING,
COUNTERATTACKING

"Boy, that's not the story we heard at the office."
"Well, there's notes in the file showing that he tried to
get things straightened out with your people."
"Hey, don't get on my case; it wasn't my fault."

This last group of roadblocks usually occurs when the buyer is upset with the listener. The customer may be hopping mad at the salesperson, and rather than feeling empathy, the sales-person feels upset, angry, and unfairly implicated. Instead of listening and helping, he gets defensive and counterattacks because now he's upset too. The result? Both parties have a grievance and nobody is listening.

These communication roadblocks are messages that represent the salesperson's thoughts, views, opinions, or advice about the customer's problem and how to solve it. They do not let the customer know that the salesperson understood the buyer. The only way to let the buyer know you have under-stood his message is to put aside your agenda and respond with active listening.

CUSTOMER COMPLAINTS

One of the main reasons that customers quit doing business with an organization is not faulty products or service but poor handling of complaints. Here are three things to remember about customers who have a complaint:

1. The story will almost always be substantially exaggerated when you first hear it.
2. The faulty product or service is generally not the most important thing in the customer's mind. What he really wants is to have his complaint heard.
3. The customer has probably incorrectly anticipated what you will say—that you will resist, argue, and so on—and has built a protective wall. Be ready for a barrage of negative replies to almost anything you say.

There are reasons customers are so often on guard and/or upset in communicating their complaints. Perhaps the cus-tomer has had a bad day in which other things have gone wrong. Perhaps something totally unrelated to your product or service has gone wrong, and when some minor problem associated with your company comes up, the customer vents all his anger at you. Or perhaps he's had the same or a similar problem before with your company, and doesn't feel he's been heard out. He will raise his temper just to make sure he gets his point across this time.

Here's an idea to remember: an irate customer asking you to look into a problem is one of the best things that can happen. That may sound downright ridiculous at first, but think about it.

First, the mere fact that the customer is expressing his anger or frustration to you indicates his confidence that you can do something about it. If he sincerely believed you could not or would not help him with his problem, he would not have complained to you in the first place. Even though it may sound negative, he's really in a hopeful and rather positive frame of mind.

Second, if the customer had no confidence in you and had kept silent about the complaint, there's a good chance that he would have "gone on down the road" and taken his business to one of your competitors. In addition, research shows he would badmouth your organization to at least twenty other people.

Whenever you hear a complaint from a customer about your company's products or services, a little red light should flash in your head signaling "Stop, look, and listen."

Stop what you are doing.
Look attentively at the customer.
Listen actively to prove your understanding of what
   the customer is saying.

When you start doing this automatically, you will be amazed at the potency of this approach. First off, it will encourage customers to ventilate all their feelings, get them out of their system. Although initially their anger may be strong, active listening will in time bring about a substantial decrease in the intensity of their feelings. What's more, sometimes active listening will help shift the subject from the flashpoint complaint to revealing an "underlying" problem, often the one that is really causing the frustration.

In any case, by using your active listening skill, you will let customers know that you are truly taking in everything they are saying. Psychologists have discovered that when people feel their strongest feelings or opinions are understood, they feel no need to keep repeating themselves, as they will when they are not understood the first time. Through your understanding of the customer's position, you are more able to help her find an appropriate solution to the problem.

Let's look at three possible scenarios that provide solutions to the customer's problem.

Scenario 1: Having vented his feelings and feeling understood, the customer comes up with a solution:

"Well, I feel better now."

"I'm glad somebody understands my complaint."

"Let's move on, everybody makes mistakes. Let's just make sure it doesn't happen again."

"Send me a new shipment and I'll return the faulty products and we'll call it even."

If the customer's solution is agreeable to you and your company, all you have to do is agree to it and see that it gets carried out.

Scenario 2: The customer doesn't come up with a solution and throws the ball to you. If your company has a standard policy, you offer that solution and hope the customer agrees to it.

Scenario 3: The customer's solution is not acceptable to you, and your solution is not acceptable to the customer. A conflict has arisen. A special win-win or no-lose approach to problem solving and conflict resolution is covered in chapter 9.

The key to all three scenarios is effective listening. It lets your customer—your partner—know that you care about his problem and that you are willing to work out a mutually acceptable solution.

OTHER PROBLEMS

There will also be times when the buyer is upset about something other than you or your company. This problem may still affect his ability to pay attention and conduct business with you. When the other person is showing signs of this, a red flag should pop up in your head. Stop what you're doing and let the buyer vent, or perhaps even solve, the problem. These problems can be personal situations like a sick family member, a son leaving home for the military, the divorce of a good friend, or a conflict at home. Or they can be problems at work like the car accident of a co-worker, his boss's recent heart attack, a sudden downturn in the market, or some new governmental regulations that will impact his job—any problem that may be troubling him and limiting his ability to focus on your conversation.

Salespeople often question if it is wise to encourage buyers to talk about their personal problems. They worry about the time it might take, and, after all, this is supposed to be a business call. But let's look at the following conversation and see what sort of results this salesperson is going to have:

SELLER: Hi, Jim, how are you doing today?

BUYER: Not worth a damn! The company just announced another cutback, and our midyear management meeting in San Francisco is out. Who knows what's next?

SELLER: Yeah, things are really tough out there. Something has to change or we'll all be on the street. Incidentally, I got something I want to show you that may save you some money on that new system you're looking at.

The buyer is upset and distracted and the seller wants to sell. That's not creating synergy in a relationship. That's having your agenda on your mind and nothing else. We'll look at how to handle that situation differently a little later.

Let me share the following personal example that illustrates the importance of listening to the buyer's problems even when they don't directly involve you or your company.

Years ago, while I (Carl Zaiss) was still in the hotel business, I was in New York calling on the meeting manager of a national insurance company. This individual booked hundreds of meetings a year in hotels and therefore represented a good deal of potential business for my company. His schedule was tight, and I had a lot of information I wanted to share with him.

Our meeting had just gotten under way when he was interrupted by a phone call from the president. It was soon very obvious that the president was very upset about something that had happened at the meeting the previous week. I motioned to the door as a way of asking if he wanted me to leave, but he shook his head that it wasn't necessary. So for almost twenty minutes I sat there in silence as he was getting chewed out. I figured I could write off this call.

After he hung up, he stared out the window for a bit and shook his head. Then he turned to me and said, "Sorry for the interruption. Where were we?"

I knew instinctively that he wasn't with me and probably wouldn't be until he got rid of the feelings about that call. So I decided to actively listen the nonverbal message I had received from him. I said, "Looks like that was a pretty unpleasant call."

He replied, "That's for sure. I booked a meeting for the president and some high-level clients in a major New York hotel last week, and everything went wrong! Just listen to what they did." And he proceeded to vent all his feelings about the hotel and the salesperson to me. Then he went on, and for the next thirty minutes this meeting planner unloaded all of his frustrations about hotels that he had stored up through the years.

It was a great learning experience for me. I came to understand the meeting planner's view of the relationship and what it meant from their side when we didn't produce what we had promised. That session was instrumental in cementing the commitment to customer satisfaction that I carried on throughout my hotel career. In addition, that meeting planner booked a lot of business in our hotels. Even though I never got the chance to "make my presentation," after our conversation *he knew that I knew what it would take to make him happy and fulfill his needs.* And that's all it takes!

If the customer has a problem, try listening. It's really as simple as that. The sales call isn't going anywhere until the buyer resolves his problems anyway. He is so preoccupied with his emotions that he is blocking out any pitch you have to make. It's time to invest in a long-term relationship.

It's essential that you listen to the buyer until one of the following four conditions are met:

1. until he vents his feelings and tells you, or signals you nonverbally by taking a deep sigh or something similar, that it's okay to continue and address the business at hand;
2. until he actually solves his own problem, which does sometimes happen, thereby eliminating the source of the feelings and readying him to continue the sales call;
3. until it becomes clear to you that the buyer is so upset that it is impossible to continue the meeting; in this case, it's time to reschedule the appointment;
4. until you find yourself in a situation where your needs aren't being met—you don't have the time or the subject matter becomes a problem for you: for example, you have another appointment to go to, or you are very uncomfortable hearing about his messy divorce; it's now time to remember your needs have to be met and asserting yourself would be appropriate.

The following examples are scripted to show two ways a conversation might go when a salesperson listens to an upset buyer. The first situation involves listening to a complaint. In this example, a restaurant manager, Chris, calls Nancy, his account executive with a uniform supplier. He is upset over the delay in his order.

SELLER: Good morning, this is Nancy Moore speaking.

CUSTOMER: Nancy, this is Chris Walker and I've got a problem. We just received our uniform order, and it's all wrong. Can't you guys do anything right?

SELLER: Chris, I'm sorry for the screwup. It sounds like we've really let you down. What happened?

CUSTOMER: You bet you did. We opened the shipping notice, and over half of the order was marked "Not available now, on back order." We're reopening next week, and I need those uniforms.

SELLER: You're concerned about the balance of the order getting there on time.

CUSTOMER: Absolutely! Look, Nancy, I knew when we decided to go with the custom design that we were operating on a tight time schedule. But you promised me we were okay four weeks ago when we checked. I don't get this back order stuff on a special order.

SELLER: Frankly, Chris, I don't either. Something's wrong. I'll check it out.

CUSTOMER: Don't just check it out, Nancy, get it resolved before my boss finds out what happened. He won't be very happy with me.

SELLER: Sounds like that would open a can of worms you don't want to have to deal with on top of everything else.

CUSTOMER: You can say that again. Listen, I never told you, but my boss was against using you from the start. Seems like you really messed him over years ago and he hasn't forgotten it. I really fought to get you in here, and the only reason he agreed was that you did have the best design. If you screw this up, I'll never hear the end of it, and he'll probably quit supporting a lot of the other changes I want to make. So get this situation straightened out.

SELLER: Chris, I appreciate the risk you took with us and the concern you have over your credibility with Frank. I will get to the bottom of this and get back to you.

Fifteen minutes later, Nancy calls back with some good news:

SELLER: Chris, it's Nancy. The balance of your order was shipped yesterday, you'll have it tomorrow. It seems that, knowing your schedule, the plant decided to get the first half to you as soon as possible. The shipping clerk didn't know the situation and just assumed the rest was on back order. I'm sorry that created such a shock for you.
CUSTOMER: That's good news. Thanks for checking it out.
SELLER: No problem, and Chris, I'll be by tomorrow to help you inventory the balance of the order and the distribution to your employees. Then after you're through the opening, I want to sit down with you and your boss and see if we can't resolve his problem with our company. I want to make sure we have everyone over there happy with us—you, your employees, and your boss.

Although the solution to that problem was simple, listening to Chris's initial barrage was not. Nancy had to truly understand the customer's feelings instead of getting defensive or otherwise throwing up roadblocks. Notice the difference if the seller had used a roadblock in her first response.

CUSTOMER: Nancy, this is Chris Walker and I've got a problem. We just received our uniform order and it's all wrong. Can't you guys do anything right?
SELLER: Oh, it can't be as bad as all that. Tell me what happened. (roadblock group #1)
[or] Don't worry, tell me what happened and I'll take care of it. (roadblock group #2)
[or] Boy, I'm beginning to wonder that myself. You're the third problem I've had this morning. (roadblock group #3)
[or] What's wrong with it? (roadblock group #4)

[*or*] I told you we were cutting the time schedule too close. (roadblock group #7)

Listening helps diffuse the customer's initial outburst, and in some cases, like this example, it allows underlying problems to surface so they, too, can be addressed.

Now let's look at a situation that requires listening to a buyer's personal problem. In this example, we'll return to the buyer who was upset over the cancellation of the management meeting.

SELLER: Hi, Jim, how are you doing today?
BUYER: Not worth a damn! The company just announced another cutback, and our midyear management meeting in San Francisco is out. Who knows what's next?
SELLER: Sounds like things are really getting tight around here.
BUYER: Yeah, but I guess it's not that bad. Business is really holding up okay for us compared to others. But the guys upstairs are using the overall economy as an excuse. They're just willy-nilly cutting back on things they don't want to do.
SELLER: So you're really questioning what they're cutting out.
BUYER: Exactly. I'm not saying we shouldn't be watching our expenses and making prudent decisions, but this meeting is an excellent vehicle for recognizing the success we have enjoyed this year and rewarding those people who have worked their buns off. I think we're missing the boat in canceling this meeting.
SELLER: In other words, you see some real value in it.
BUYER: You bet I do. And the other thing is that people were looking at this meeting as a chance to address some of the obstacles in our quality improvement program. They'll interpret canceling the meeting as a lack of commitment to the new program. You know, like quality is okay as long as it doesn't cost us anything.
SELLER: I know exactly what you mean. It looks as if upper

management's decisions are inconsistent with what they say they are committed to.

BUYER: Yep, you got it. (silence) But I just got why I'm really upset.

SELLER: Oh?

BUYER: Yeah, my wife's going to be real disappointed. She was coming on the trip with me and was going to spend some time with our daughter in San Jose while I was in meetings. Then on Friday we were going to drive up to the Napa Valley for the weekend, and fly home Monday. Boy, telling her isn't going to be easy.

SELLER: That's a conversation you're not looking forward to.

BUYER: Yeah, that's true. But that's tonight. Sorry I spouted off so much. Let's look at those numbers you brought over to review.

By allowing the buyer to vent his feelings, the salesperson can now get down to the business at hand with a buyer who is focused on the conversation. More important, the salesperson demonstrated his concern for the buyer and the importance of the relationship—not just the business side of it. As it turned out, the buyer didn't want to bare his soul, just get it off his chest. In this case, the salesperson expended a few minutes that possibly cemented a stronger relationship.

As a comparison, review the roadblocks again and look at the effects on the communication flow that a roadblock would have created. Then return to the thought we heard at the beginning of the chapter:

I don't care how much you know until I know how much you care.

Chapter Summary

1. The three primary areas in which to use the listening skills during the selling/buying process are
   - when listening for the buyer's unmet needs and

fears in Step 1 of the buyer's decision-making process;

- when listening to the buyer's resistance to change;
- when listening to the buyer's complaints and/or problems.

2. Pitfalls to avoid in Step 1 of the buyer's decision-making process are
   - controlling the conversation through leading questions;
   - forcing the buyer to defend her position by asking "why" questions;
   - judging and evaluating what the buyer is saying;
   - moving into the selling mode after hearing a buying signal.

3. To facilitate the change process an effective salesperson will
   - understand and accept the buyer's feelings about the change process through the use of active listening;
   - avoid the "fix-it" mentality;
   - listen to uncover core issues about the change.

4. Communication roadblocks impede the problem-solving process and have a negative impact on the relationship. When the roadblocks arc used, the other person does not feel heard or understood.

5. When responding to a customer complaint, it is important to
   - *stop* what you are doing;
   - *look* attentively at the customer;
   - *listen* actively to prove your understanding of what the customer is saying.

6. Listening to a customer problem
   - proves you care about her problem;
   - gets to core issues that need to be resolved;
   - sets the stage for effective problem solving.

CHAPTER SIX

HOW TO BREAK THROUGH

TO NEW LEVELS

OF SELF-EXPRESSION

To thine own self be true.

—*SHAKESPEARE*

Real communication is obviously easiest when one person believes that the other will freely accept what he says or does. Being authentic is more difficult when we risk disagreement, resistance, judgments, or even criticism from others. We constantly weigh the risks versus the rewards as we question possible options. Can I tell my customer how I really feel about her decision or about her being late for our meetings? Can I speak up at sales meetings without others feeling I'm a troublemaker, or can I tell my boss exactly how I feel about the new compensation package without affecting my annual performance evaluation? Can I say no to a customer when his request conflicts with my personal values? Can I speak up in my company to get my customer's needs satisfied and not risk upsetting someone I have to deal with on a daily basis? These are difficult and sometimes frightening decisions to make. All the same, the potential benefits of being more authentic are overwhelming—both for yourself and for your relationships with others.

The most obvious benefit, of course, is that you will like yourself better. Authenticity breeds greater self-confidence and respect. You will feel better about yourself not only as a salesperson but also as a person. When you are open, honest, and clear with people, you'll feel stronger, more responsible, and confident.

When you're authentic, others get a more accurate reading of who you really are. Your customers will know what's important to you in your dealing with them; they won't be in the dark about where you stand on certain issues. Uncertainty will be replaced by an accurate awareness of who you really are and what you stand for.

This is important in building partnerships. Being open and direct invariably encourages the same from your customers and others around you. This facilitates the development of trust between two people, and in sales, trust is an essential ingredient of success. Trust is developed when the salesperson is seen as natural and genuine, without a front or a façade. Take off the mask of the professional salesperson and allow the real you to emerge.

Authenticity can be a difficult concept for people to grasp at times. Everyone can relate to the proper adjectives like *real*, *natural*, and *genuine*. But deeper issues are involved in the context of selling in the new synergistic model. Authenticity also includes thinking for yourself and allowing yourself to get away from the automatic-pilot effect that your training created. Remember, your past conditioning forms your personal paradigms, your belief systems. These paradigms determine your behavior. They shape what you think, what you say, and what you don't say.

These paradigms develop early in life. Many people remember being told, "Don't speak unless spoken to" and "Children should be seen and not heard." We were criticized for crying, yelling, screaming, and hitting other children, and we get the message that *self-expression of any kind is not acceptable.*

When we went to school, self-expression was rarely encouraged. Our self-expression in the form of homework or projects was graded and judged by others. Talk about stifling! Groups of twenty to thirty children were herded into groups, and those who didn't fit were sent to the principal's office. Our education system is another example of a dying paradigm, one that doesn't work anymore and is in need of a major paradigm shift. Self-expression and authenticity are seldom encouraged during the years at school.

When we went to work, the message was the same: "Don't make waves" or "Keep your nose to the grindstone." A participant in one of our recent programs reported that his current boss told him "My way or the highway!" And many salespeople hear, "The customer is always right." The message is the same: play by the rules, do what you're told, don't ask questions, be professional, don't let your feelings show, and so on.

Throughout our entire lives, our individual self-expression has been discouraged and suppressed. You bring that history to this chapter, which addresses a whole new level of authentic behavior. During the Synergistic Selling course, the participants complete an exercise that illustrates how their conditioning limits authentic communication and impacts their effectiveness in dealing with others. In this exercise, people are asked to identify someone inside their organization who is causing a problem in getting something done for a customer. Next, the participants are instructed to script how they think the conversation would go with that person if they confronted him about the problem. Finally, they are told to write down in the margin what they are thinking but not saying to the other person during the conversation. Here's a typical example of that exercise.

* * *

Problem identification: I am having a problem with Mark, the sales support manager, because he does not get back to me on a timely basis with information for my customers.

The script of the expected conversation ran as follows:

1. ME: Mark, I've called three times to get that custom design layout I need for the XYZ client. What's going on over there?
2. MARK: Look, Tom, I got your messages, and I'm sorry, but we're just swamped in here. That new marketing program has loaded us down.
3. ME: Well, it's nice to hear business is so great. So have you got the revisions to the design I need for my customer?
4. MARK: Not yet, but I'll get back to you by four o'clock today.
5. ME: Can I count on that?
6. MARK: Yeah, if I can track down Johnson. He'll need to review the final design and approve it.
7. ME: Mark, look, no games. Track down Johnson and get me the new design today. Okay?
8. MARK: Okay.

In the margin, the participant wrote the following for what he was thinking but not saying to Mark.

1. Well, he finally answered his phone. Probably forgot to turn his voice mail on.
2. You guys are always swamped. I've never seen such confusion in my life. It's harder to get information out of my own home office than from my clients.
3. I'm feeling put off again.
4. What do you mean "if you can track down Johnson"? His office is just down the hall!
5. You don't get it! I'm out here busting my buns to bring us business, and I've got a client who has to work to do business with us. We should be taking care of his needs. Why does this have to be so difficult?

After completing the exercise, one of the most interesting discussions in the Synergistic Selling course occurs in answer to this question: "What stops you from speaking the unspoken comments in the margin?" Participants share the following answers: "It might upset the other person," "It might start a conflict," "I have to work with that person every day," "They might get back at me somehow."

Because of the possible consequences of upsetting the other person, people don't share what they are really thinking during a conversation. This fear stems from their past conditioning and their resulting paradigms about relating to others. This is a great example of the impact of the win-lose paradigm that influences our lives so much. Virtually no one sees how we can speak up to get our needs met and at the same time make sure the other person doesn't lose in the process. Even the fear that being honest will cause a conflict comes from our past experiences that someone wins and someone loses when people get into a conflict. Therefore, we tend to avoid conflicts at all cost.

Several lessons can be learned from this classroom exercise on unspoken communication. First of all, not speaking up runs counter to your desire to serve your client. When we ask the participants of our course to raise their hands if they are committed to customer satisfaction, every single one of them will do so. But who loses in the long run when internal problems such as the one in the example above don't get resolved? The customer.

Participants look stunned when they become aware that they are more committed to being nice to each other and avoiding unpleasant conversations than they are to satisfying customers. Then they get defensive and come up with dozens of other ways to handle the problem. Order him to solve the problem in the name of customer satisfaction, go around him, go to your boss, and so on. Everyone has their own strategy for dealing with obstacles within the company. All come from the win-lose mentality that permeates and cripples our relationships with others. Rarely does "Tell him how you feel" come up as an option.

It is important that salespeople realize the impact of this. When things go wrong or don't get done, we blame others rather than accept our responsibility of speaking up. Look at how you and the people in your life shift the blame, and yet things don't change. The same problems and situations come up time and again. It's because the conversations that could get to the heart of problems remain unspoken.

A second lesson to learn is that we aren't telling the truth in our communication with others. Participants get upset when they hear this. Everyone likes to think they tell the truth. But in reality people usually say what is acceptable at the time. And "acceptable" is determined by the limited thinking of the traditional win-lose paradigm.

The actual implications are, among other things, that you are being disrespectful. Actually, you are communicating that the other person isn't worth the risk or that you don't trust them to handle what you have to say. You are closing down the opportunity to build an effective relationship with the other person, inasmuch as these unspoken thoughts continue to grow and block the communications between you. It's actually the unspoken communication between two people that influences the quality of the relationship more than what is said. Think about it for a moment, and look at the implications for your relationships.

You are not expressing your real needs, so you won't have them met. You end up a loser. Losers resent winners, and that resentment toward the other person usually manifests itself in some way.

Being authentic is a trait that enhances relationships and enhances your feelings of self-worth. Yet therein lies an interesting paradox. On the one hand, ask people what they value from others in a relationship, and they'll reply that they respect directness and honesty. They make positive comments like "You always know where he's coming from" or "There's no hidden agendas with Sally" or "Jim's a straight shooter." But when they're asked to be open themselves, people hesitate—they're afraid of what others will think.

The third lesson is that getting out from behind your

mask and becoming a real person with real problems and feelings will enhance your relationships. Psychologists call this "being congruent." Your inner thoughts and feelings match what you show or share with others—in other words, it's speaking the unspoken in the exercise above.

Carl R. Rogers, in his book *On Becoming a Person*, expresses it this way: "The greater the congruence of experience, awareness and communication on the part of one individual, the more the ensuing relationship will involve: a tendency toward reciprocal communication with a quality of increasing congruence; a tendency toward more mutually accurate understanding of the communications; mutual satisfaction in the relationship."

An experience from our Synergistic Selling classes illustrates the value of congruent communications in a more tangible way. The situation occurred in a sales-training course for the AC Delco division of General Motors, conducted by Carl Zaiss. One of the participants, Sam, asked me, "Don't you think that there are times a power close is needed to get people to make a decision?" I replied that I didn't think it was ever an appropriate action if it was interpreted by the buyer as coercion or manipulation. Sam disagreed, and what followed was a Ping-Pong match over who was right. I felt his resistance increasing, and finally he said, "Well, have you ever called on one of our distributors?" I said, "Yes, I have, and I'm convinced that they are looking for a win-win outcome also and would resent the pressure of a power close." That ended the discussion and the group started a written exercise.

During this time, I noticed that I was feeling really uncomfortable with the interaction with Sam. I realized I had not listened to his concern, but reacted very defensively. I decided to share those thoughts when the group reconvened. I began by apologizing to Sam and then confessed that I was uncomfortable with the interaction. Sam, in turn, acknowledged that he felt he was pushing me into a corner just to look good in front of the group. I asked the group if anyone had noticed what had happened; several said they felt that I had gotten defensive and countered Sam's beliefs instead of understanding them. What ensued was a discussion on the value of the listening skills that brought home their true impact. The conversation turned out to be a major learning experience for many of the participants and would not have occurred if I had not taken a risk and communicated my inner thoughts.

Salespeople who take off their professional salesperson mask and become more congruent in their communication pave the way for the buyer to do the same. The result is more honest two-way communication and more effective buying decisions. And that means greater customer satisfaction.

Communicating the unspoken and being more authentic with buyers and others does require taking a risk. But that risk can be greatly diminished by learning how to send self-disclosing messages.

Effective Self-Disclosure

Saying what you feel is a powerful and stimulating way of communicating. Yet past programming limits most people to only two options, being unassertive or being aggressive. Typically, people's behavior and communication fall roughly into one of those two categories.

Unassertive behavior means not communicating your honest feelings, needs, or values; or expressing them in such a self-effacing way that other people ignore them. Unassertive people go to great lengths to avoid conflict with others. They subordinate their needs to those of others and often end up angry, frustrated, and resentful.

Because unassertive people are often disregarded or ignored, this then reinforces their belief that they aren't important. It becomes a self-fulfilling prophecy.

Most common among unassertive people is the "nice guy" or "sweet lady" syndrome. These people subordinate their needs because of their conditioning in the traditional win-lose paradigm. Nice guys or sweet ladies believe the only other option to "nice" is "not nice." They limit their behavior possibilities to unassertive or aggressive.

Examples of unassertive behavior are very common in the field of sales. One reason for this is that most of us don't want to come across as the typical, pushy, salesperson and often swing to the opposite extreme. But, in fact, when a salesperson is unassertive, what he's really telling his customers is, "I'm not important and therefore what I have to say isn't important either."

Aggressive behavior, on the other hand means getting one's needs met but often at the expense of others. Aggressive people openly communicate their needs and opinions, but in a way that usually puts down the other person. Simply put, aggressive people are insensitive to the needs of others. Not all aggressive behavior is blatant, however. Some people satisfy their needs at the expense of others through manipulation, sabotage, or silent, stubborn resistance.

To most people unassertiveness and aggressiveness are their only options. Their conditioning limits them to the either/or thinking. Because of this, many people tend to be unassertive until their resentment boils over, and then they switch to aggressive behavior. Likewise, some people are aggressive until feelings of guilt take over, and they then become passive. That has been the basis for selling in the past. You can't afford to be weak (the loser), so you must be strong (the winner). That is the consequence of the traditional win-lose paradigm.

There is, however, a third option, one critical to the development of synergistic relationships. This is assertive behavior. Assertive people know what they want and communicate these desires effectively, but in ways that do not violate the rights of others. They are open, authentic, and congruent with their inner feelings.

The best way to communicate assertively to others is through the use of "I-Messages." This is a congruent message reflecting the actual nature and strength of your thoughts and feelings. It is a clear message, understandable, and to the point, not masked by indirect or vague language.

Let's look at the various types of I-Messages.

DECLARATIVE I-MESSAGE

This form of self-expression declares to others your beliefs, ideas, likes, dislikes, feelings, thoughts, and reactions. Examples of this include

"I believe that a demonstration of our equipment is the only way to really see its benefits."

"I would like you to sit in on this meeting. Your input would be valuable."

"I suggest you also consider the Model 2403. It may fit your requirements and is less expensive."

PREVENTIVE I-MESSAGE

Another important type of self-disclosure is one that announces what you want to do, or see happen, in the future. Such a message, because it clearly describes how you want events to turn out, greatly increases the chances that others will adjust what they do to help you meet your needs. A Preventive I-Message goes something like this: "I would like _____, because _____." For example:

"I would like to start our meeting right at two and end at three, because I have a tight schedule today."

"I'd like to know your reorder requirements today because we need to work out a realistic delivery schedule."

"I need to know your conference schedule by Thursday, because I need to inform our other departments."

RESPONSIVE I-MESSAGE

This is an effective way to say no when another person asks us to do something we can't do. Customers can make a lot of demands on your time, energy, and resources. Anxiety often grips us as we listen to these requests, for we fear the consequences of our refusal. We feel under pressure, and perhaps genuinely confused about whether to say yes or no. When we do say yes instead of an honest no, we have not communicated our needs and feel down on ourselves and resentful of the customer for making the request. These are times when building synergistic partnerships can be a challenge.

Many salespeople find themselves unable to say no to a customer's request. Here are some of the main reasons why:

"I might lose the sale." Obviously, salespeople want to make sales and keep customers, so it's natural that they fear doing anything that might upset the customer.

"I want to be a good guy." One of the earliest lessons taught us as children, and still reinforced in many ways as adults, is the idea that we should be nice to other people—unselfish, charitable, generous. Turning someone down who seems in need, or who seems to be acting generously toward us, creates a lot of guilt and tension.

"I'll get rewarded in kind." Salespeople often operate on the belief that if they say yes to a customer now, she will feel obligated to give them the business.

"The customer is always right." I am continually amazed by how many salespeople genuinely believe that selling requires them to compromise, make sacrifices, and always give the benefit of the doubt to the customer. In the traditional paradigm, self-sacrifice simply goes with the territory.

Naturally, many times you feel perfectly comfortable saying yes to a request. It's when you don't want to say yes that the skill of assertive communication comes in. If you can successfully say no, you have acted to prevent resentment and other feelings that later are detrimental to you and to the partnership.

Responsive I-Messages are effective because they contain two important elements. The first is "your decision." This is a statement of declining a request such as, "No, I don't want to," "I have decided not to," or "I'm choosing not to." It is important to avoid saying "I can't" or "I won't be able to" and similar phrases that suggest that you are not in control of your life. As mentioned earlier, assertiveness means taking personal responsibility and choosing what you want to do. An assertive response like "I don't want to" leaves no doubt that you are the source of the decision. A response like "I just can't" inevitably produces the reply "Why not?" You are now in a defensive position and must own up to the decision or retreat further into excuses.

Such a frank answer must be followed, however, by your convincing reasons. Someone will accept a no answer much more readily if they clearly understand your reasons. Giving common-sense reasons also eliminates doubt that you are being arbitrary, uncooperative, or worse, that you don't really care about the customer. The more concrete the reason is, the better. A vague reason like "I'm too busy" is not as convincing as "I have three meetings already scheduled that I don't want to change." When people hear reasons that they can imagine in their own lives, they are much more understanding.

Let's look at some examples of Responsive I-Messages:

"Thanks for the lunch offer, Jerry, but I don't want to today. I have an important meeting in an hour, and I want to do some preparation."

"No, Tom, I don't want to reschedule my vacation for that meeting. We have nonrefundable tickets and confirmed hotel reservations."

"No, Sally, I've decided not to fax the proposal to you today. I'm still waiting on some figures from our pricing department."

"No, Tom, I decided not to fly to New York next week. I've got our national sales meeting to prepare for."

APPRECIATIVE I-MESSAGE

One of the most enriching forms of self-disclosure, this message describes your positive feelings toward your customers,

co-workers, or others. When people are especially consider-
ate, or say a good word when it's needed most, you should
express your thanks to them.

The Appreciative I-Message is a genuine, no-strings-
attached expression of feelings. It is not deliberate, manipulative flattery in order to get something out of the other person.
Nothing turns the other person off faster than insincere, re-
hearsed sweet talk. On the other hand, genuine expressions of
gratitude go a long way toward keeping a relationship strong
overall and full of mutual goodwill.

Participants tell us they worry about being wimpy or un-
professional. Yet this is a powerful tool for building the kind
of relationships required in sales today. It is a strong statement about who you are and what you value, and it definitely
gets heard by the other person. Sadly, positive messages of
this type are so rare in our culture that they stand out. Examples of Appreciative I-Messages include

> "Bob, I really appreciated your flexibility on the
> delivery schedule. We had some internal problems
> that caused some delays."

> "Marilyn, I appreciate the prompt and profes-
> sional manner in which you get back to me. It saves
> me a lot of time and frustration."

> "Joan, thanks for arranging the special session
> with your staff. I think it will help the installation go
> more smoothly."

CONFRONTIVE I-MESSAGE

This comes into play when you are experiencing a problem
brought on by the behavior of a customer or someone else.
Remember, you have rights too. This is the only way to create
the balance inherent in a synergistic relationship. Let's face it,
the old adage that "the customer is always right" just doesn't
hold up anymore. Although customers may not do it intention-

ally, they do take actions (or inactions) that lead to real trouble for the salesperson. So salespeople often end up feeling very disadvantaged in their relationships with certain customers. Most of you have had customers who keep you waiting for appointments or fail to show up at all; who "forget" to furnish you with promised information necessary for your sales proposal; who make demands on your time that are excessive and unfair; or who may treat you with disrespect and show little concern for your needs.

Traditionally, sales organizations have required their personnel to set aside their own needs and feelings and do whatever it takes to keep the customer happy. In short, salespeople have played the "I lose-you win" game in order to ultimately "win" by getting the sale. There are real risks for salespeople who fail to stand up for their rights and legitimate needs.

One way that salespeople have traditionally handled being put upon (or have been trained to do so) is denying or suppressing their unhappiness. This grin-and-bear-it approach works at times; however, you run the risk of simply delaying the inevitable. One day, after too many rounds of losing to the customer, you may unload all of that pent-up resentment. Or, you may begin to withdraw from the customer, or go on the attack in subtle, indirect ways like being late for appointments or "forgetting" to handle a complaint call. Salespeople who continue to lose with customers also take out their resentment on others around them or even leave their job out of frustration. The bottom line of the grin-and-bear-it approach is a strategy for the win-lose model that in the long run doesn't work for anyone.

In the synergistic model, salespeople have three choices to consider when dealing with a customer who is creating a problem for them. It's important to make clear that we are talking here about a customer behavior that is creating a concrete problem for the salesperson, behavior that is interfering with the salesperson being able to get her needs met.

DEALING WITH PROBLEM BEHAVIOR

CHOICE ONE: ACCEPT THINGS AS THEY ARE

As discussed earlier, acceptance of any sort of customer behavior has been the traditional response by many salespeople. And let's be realistic: there are situations when you are willing to put up with just about anything because the stakes are so high. This is a legitimate choice to make: begrudging but necessary acceptance of the customer's actions.

There is another kind of acceptance, however, that is not begrudging. This is a philosophical acceptance of the way things are and will likely always be. You've probably had a close personal relationship which you valued so much that you decided to no longer be bothered by some idiosyncrasy of the other person; you grew to realize that this is simply the way this person is and nothing will ever change that fact. And has it ever happened that the very behavior or habit that you decided to accept actually became something you liked because it added to the charm or individuality of this special person?

Here are some questions you can ask yourself that could lead to a willing acceptance of a customer's irritating behavior:

- Is there room enough in this world for me, the way I am, and this customer, the way she is?
- Why does this customer's behavior bother me? Does it bother my sensibilities or values, but not tangibly affect me? Is it really that important?
- Can I take the view that as a salesperson I will have to deal with every type of human being imaginable and that greater, not lesser, tolerance will make my life as a salesperson more enjoyable and productive?
- Am I perhaps too thin-skinned, too defensive in my role as a salesperson, perhaps harboring a sense of inferiority or low status because I am in selling?

To correct this, can I increase my pride and self-respect as a salesperson so that I don't "bleed" with every little scratch?

If you can answer yes to one or more of those questions, acceptance can be a legitimate, healthy way of responding to some of the problems customers cause in your life.

CHOICE TWO: CHANGE YOURSELF IF YOU ARE PART OF THE PROBLEM

In a world in which too many people, cultures, and nations are quick to point the finger of blame, there is great value in self-examination when one of your relationships goes a little sour. The adage that there are always two sides to a problem is often very true. This suggests that, before trying to change the other person, you might want to change yourself; in the process, you may discover that it's actually your behavior that is triggering the other person's behavior that you don't like. Take, for example, the salesperson who is always vague about when he will visit a customer, communicating the idea that time really isn't that vulnerable. This salesperson typically says, "I'll drop in on Monday or Tuesday." Then when the salesperson has to tighten up his schedule and start making appointments, who is to blame when the customer isn't available at the appointed time? Another example is the salesperson who always brushes aside one customer's questions and minor complaints about the product, never really listening to her customer's feelings, and then hears that this customer has given a very critical evaluation of her product to a potential customer. Should the salesperson feel betrayed or deceived, or did she build her own trap?

Being authentic requires honest introspection. Here are some questions you can ask yourself in an effort to find out whether you're part of the problem you're having with some of your customers:

- Is there something about me that brings on the behavior I don't like? Do I set the other person up to then let them down?
- "If so, am I willing to change that behavior so that I'm not contributing to the problem?
- "Am I doing enough to maintain a good relationship with this person? Am I servicing the customer the way I should, or am I taking the account for granted? Are the irritating things this customer is doing merely symptoms of a dissatisfied customer who needs some prompt attention?

A long thoughtful look in the mirror may lead you to say, "I've met the enemy and it is me."

CHOICE THREE: TRY TO CHANGE THE CUSTOMER

Finally, if you can't accept the customer's behavior and are unwilling or unable to change yourself, you can attempt to change the person who's causing you a problem. This could well be your first choice; it is listed here as the third only because of the inherent risks in trying to change someone. Actually, you can't do it anyway. Only the other person can really choose to change. All you can do is create the climate and opportunity for change. This is especially true for salespeople; rarely do they have any actual control over their customers. What they can do is attempt to influence their customers to change out of consideration for the salesperson's rights and needs.

Even under the best of circumstances, efforts to change someone run predictable risks. The other person may feel criticized or blamed; she may get defensive and refuse to listen; you may get confronted in return; the relationship may become strained.

On the other hand, the outcome may be very positive. The customer appreciates hearing your concerns and readily cooperates in changing (perhaps along with some changes in you too), and the relationship grows even stronger, with greater mutual respect.

Again, here are some questions to ask yourself:

- Is this customer's behavior one which I simply cannot accept? Have I really thought through why I have a problem with this person? How am I actually being hurt by this behavior? Or is it just a difference in values or style between us? And is that important to me?
- Can this customer possibly change? Am I confronting something that is too deeply ingrained in this person? Or is their behavior actually under the control of someone else (like their boss)? If so, is there someone else I should confront?
- Am I willing and able to deal with the person's reactions to me—their possible anger, embarrassment, defensiveness?
- If I confront this person, am I open to the possibility that I too might have to change because of what I learn about my own role in creating the problem?

Whether you decide to accept, change yourself, or confront will of course depend on many considerations. The important point is to consciously choose, not to simply hope the problem will go away or to fall back into automatic pilot and do what you've always done because you have "no choice." You have the right to self-respect, professional integrity, and human dignity, just as your customer does, and everyone else for that matter.

CONFRONTING YOUR CUSTOMER

Confronting a customer, letting him know that you don't like something they have done, is not an easy decision. It involves risk. Yet it may be the thing you feel you must do.

Let's say, for example, that the problem is a customer who consistently keeps you waiting for appointments, sometimes thirty minutes or more. Twice in the last month, he has actually forgotten and not even been in town when you called on him. Further, let's assume that these delayed or missed sales calls are costing you a lot of wasted travel time and lost opportunities to do other work. On the other hand, this tardy customer is a very good account. Let's further imagine that you've considered the alternatives—acceptance of the customer's action or making a change yourself—and decided instead to try to influence the customer to change. In fact, you've sent Preventive I-Messages, but they haven't worked. You are now feeling very upset, and you can't go on until you get some relief from the problem.

When you decide to confront a customer, or any other person for that matter, there are three goals you should try to achieve. First, you want to get relief from the problem, usually through a change in the customer's actions. Second, you want to preserve the customer's self-esteem and pride. Third, you want to keep the relationship intact, even improving it if possible.

Many people, when they are upset at someone, think only about the first goal—relief for themselves. But the salesperson who wants to maintain a synergistic relationship with her customer must be equally concerned about minimizing any adverse effects on the other person.

Confrontive I-Messages can influence customers to change. Remember that an I-Message is simply an honest, direct expression of your thoughts and feelings; it tells the truth about what you are experiencing at a given moment. The Confrontive I-Message is a special type of self-disclosure that communicates three important pieces of information: (1) a nonblameful description of what the customer is saying or doing that is creating a problem for you; (2) the specific unwanted effects that the behavior is causing you; and (3) the strength of your feelings about those ill effects on you.

For a Confrontive I-Message to work, the other person must understand clearly how you are being adversely affected and then initiate change in his behavior out of consideration for you. Even when people don't know each other very well or have a highly temporary relationship, they will usually show consideration because they can identify with your problem—that is, they can put themselves in your shoes. They most likely will choose to do for you what they want others to do for them—change their interfering behavior.

Let's look at some examples of effective confrontations based on this three-part I-Message. First, read the three elements, then the complete I-Message.

In the first example, the customer we discussed earlier is always late for an appointment and yesterday you were late for a very important meeting as a result of his being late. A good Confrontive I-Message might be

"Bill, when you are late for our appointments, it messes up my schedule and I run late for other meetings. I may have even lost a big order yesterday because I was late following our meeting. I'm really frustrated with this situation."

In a second example, a customer has not mailed you the specs you need to give her a bid. She claims to be interested in your products but forgets to follow up on her agreements. This has happened two weeks in a row, and the deadline for submitting proposals is rapidly approaching. In this case, a good Confrontive I-Message might be

"Ms. Jones, twice now you've said you would mail the specs and they haven't arrived. I'm getting concerned that I'll not get the quote to you before the deadline."

Notice that each of these Confrontive I-Messages was put together a little differently; in the first example, the order of the three parts was: Behavior-Effects-Feelings. In the second example it was Behavior-Feelings-Effect. The order of these parts just isn't that important. The point here is that the form of the I-Message isn't what's important; it's the content that counts.

Here are some guidelines for making your confrontations effective.

PART 1. BEHAVIOR

Do describe the other's behavior in enough detail so that it's clear exactly what you don't like (e.g., "when you haven't sent the specs for the new uniform design").

Don't describe vague and general behavior (e.g., "when you don't follow up").

Don't add words that blame, criticize, or exaggerate (e.g., "when you procrastinate").

Don't try to analyze why. You can't really know the person's motives or intentions anyway (e.g., "when you keep putting off sending me the design").

PART 2. CONCRETE EFFECTS

Do describe exactly how you are being adversely affected; emphasize the practical effects—those that another can easily identify with (e.g., "I lose time," "miss sales calls" "spend extra money," etc.).

Don't be vague about the effects or leave them out (e.g., "It's kind of a problem," "messes me up," etc.).

PART 3. FEELINGS ABOUT EFFECTS

Do describe your feelings of displeasure, irritation, fear, and frustration as you are actually experiencing them. Let the other person hear the actual strength of those feelings. Try to connect the feeling to the effect. Say "I'm worried about missing the deadline" rather than "I'm worried."

Don't leave out the feelings, since they let the other person know how much you care about the effects of his behavior.

Don't exaggerate your feelings by being melodramatic; on the other hand, don't hold back either. Be authentic.

* * *

Before going on, let's address the issue of anger. When another's behavior causes you a problem, your first feeling might be that of anger or hostility. Anger, however, is often the result of another underlying feeling. For example, if you are driving on the freeway and someone's driving nearly causes you to have an accident, you may react initially with anger: "Watch out, you stupid idiot!" Yet a moment later you may become aware of the primary feeling at work—namely, fear. "That near miss really scared me!" Therefore, in sending Confrontive I-Messages, try to get in touch with your primary feelings and express them to the other person.

Not only are primary feelings more accurate, but avoiding expression of anger will also avoid a possible defensive response by the other person. Nearly everyone feels empathy toward another's fear, worry, or frustration; not so with anger, especially when directed at them.

YOU-MESSAGES DON'T WORK

Whereas the idea of an I-Message may seem sensible, many of us fail to confront in this way. Rather we often communicate in "You-Messages." We talk about "you—over there" instead of "I—over here" and thus fail to communicate what we're really feeling.

You-Messages express judgments, guesses, labels, and commands or threats. Since no one likes to be branded or told what to do, You-Messages generally create hurt feelings, defensiveness, and resistance in others. No customer likes to have a finger pointed at her and be told, "You really screwed up," "You are inconsiderate," "You evidently don't care how long you keep me waiting," "You better get me that material or I can't promise delivery."

The four most common You-Messages are:

THE PUT-DOWN

This message blames, criticizes, scolds, or moralizes. It is designed to punish along with pointing out the problem you are having (e.g., "Do you think it's right to keep me waiting like you do?").

THE LABEL

Here the message directly evaluates, labels, or types the customer in some general negative way (e.g., "You are inconsiderate of others").

THE THREAT

Subtly or blatantly, this message suggests some unpleasant consequence (e.g., "You're not going to get the best price if you don't get the design specs back to me sooner").

THE ORDER

This confrontation message gives a direct order or strongly suggests how the customer should change, rather than letting them initiate change in their own way (e.g., "Please go get those specs and put them in the mail").

The Confrontive I-Message works well because it lets the person know in no uncertain terms how her behavior is hurting you. And because this kind of confrontation does not order, direct, or threaten, customers feel that they have a choice about how they will respond. Since you aren't demanding change, there is nothing to be resisted. Rather, a sense of responsibility is created in the other person, leading to a decision, in most cases, to help you out.

Here's an example that shows how it works. This one involves a participant who, after our program, confronted her boss, the general manager of a hotel. He called to report the story as he was pleased to see the skills in action, getting results. Following the training session, Pattie, the front office manager, went to her boss's office to discuss a problem she was having. She said she wanted to try something she had learned in the class, and he said go right ahead. She took a deep breath and said: "When you come through the front office between 8:00 and 8:30 each morning the staff gets real nervous. That is their busiest time of the day, and they think you're checking on their performance. I get very worried that your presence slows down our service and efficiency."

Pattie had delivered a sound Confrontive I-Message. The general manager felt a need to be out with the employees letting them know he cared about them. The timing of the trip through the front office didn't matter. He told Pattie that he appreciated her bringing the situation to his attention and that he would avoid peak hours on his walk-throughs. This turned out to have been an easy situation, and many are, in fact, easier than you think they'll be. However, that is not always the case. No one likes to be confronted, to be told something they have done is causing a problem for someone else. Guilt and embarrassment, to some degree, overtake all of us when we become aware of our shortcomings. At other times, we may vehemently deny any wrongdoing or feel perfectly justified in our actions.

One thing is nearly certain: a person who is confronted will experience some form of unpleasant or uncomfortable reaction. You-Messages, of course, produce a lot of this. But even a textbook-perfect Confrontive I-Message will result in some degree of unpleasantness for the other person. Because of this, confrontation is not enough. Something must be done to deal with the other person's inevitable reaction.

From chapter 6 you will recall the value of listening to the customer when he is experiencing a problem. So you now need to "shift gears" from confronting to helping the customer deal with his reaction to your I-Message. The listening skills, and especially active listening, now become the appropriate response. In fact, if you don't shift gears to listen to the customer and instead repeat or amplify your confrontive message, the problem will likely get even worse.

The key to shifting gears is active listening. The shift from asserting to listening sends a very important message: "I see that what I have said made you upset. I want to hear and understand your concerns." Listening then gives the other a vent for her feelings and provides a climate for effective resolution of the conflict. The process of listening, with its display of concern for the other, is often sufficient to lower resistance so that you can shift gears again and return to clarify or expand your confrontation. In fact, you may shift gears back and forth several times—confronting, listening, confronting, listening, and so on—until some resolution is achieved or until the true issues in the conflict are defined, which sets the stage for the conflict-resolution process.

Let's examine an example of shifting gears. In this scenario, Debra, a saleswoman for a printing company, decides to confront her customer on the delays in getting the approved proofs returned. Notice how she shifts to active listening after the initial Confrontive-I Message and where she reasserts herself.

SELLER (1): John, hi, it's Debra. I've got a problem. When you refuse to review and approve a new set of proofs, I get concerned about meeting the deadline on your project and we're also tying up our presses for your run. We end up having to slow down our production on other projects.

BUYER: Look, Debra, I called the changes over to Laurie yesterday, and we're swamped over here getting everything else ready for the new product presentation. The brochure is just one of my concerns.

SELLER (2): John, I hear that you're really on a fast pace and that you've got a lot going on in addition to the brochure. I'm also aware you called over the changes, but you know I can't start the presses until we get a new set of approved proofs.

BUYER: Debra, ever since they dropped this project on me a month ago to have ready for the annual sales meeting, things have gone wrong. The new product photography didn't come out, my creative people changed the copy, and the president added a special incentive for the sales-people that I had to write up and develop a campaign for. All this and the meeting's next week.

SELLER (3): So you're really feeling pressured.

BUYER: That's right, and I have to take a shortcut wherever I can.

SELLER (4): From where you stand, then, approving and sign-ing a new set of proofs is a step you can save since you've already called in some changes.

BUYER: That's right.

SELLER (5): Okay, John, I got that. But here's my concern. This project is too important for a screwup and it's been rushed. I don't want to run the risk of Laurie's misinter-preting what you said over the phone. I'm concerned that one little mistake could jeopardize the quality of accu-racy of the brochure, and it's too important for your company to take that risk. In addition, I don't want to start the run on this size project until you've signed off on it.

BUYER: Debra, the changes weren't that major. There shouldn't be any confusion.

SELLER (6): John, I really hear that the changes are not enough to warrant another set of proofs. Yet I've seen smaller changes be misunderstood and the client be upset with the final product. I don't want to take that risk in this situation.

BUYER: Okay, what do you suggest? I go into a meeting in an hour with the production company reviewing next week's schedule and it could take the rest of the day.

SELLER (7): How does this sound? To save you time, I'll per-sonally review the new set of proofs and then bring them over this afternoon at one o'clock. I request that you take a twenty-to-thirty-minute break in the meeting, and then you and I can go through the changes together to make sure they are what you want. That way I can still get you on the presses today.

BUYER: All right, Debra, maybe you're right. I'll see you at one.

In her opening, #1, Debra sends a very direct and effective I-Message, and then in #2 she responds with active listening, proving she's understood John's concern. Responses #3 and #4 are again active listening that shows she thoroughly understands the problem from John's point of view. Then in #5, Debra asserts herself again to make sure John understands what she needs and why. Then in #6 she replies with an active-listening response to let John know she understood him and then clarifies her own position. Finally, in #7 she responds to John's request for a solution with one she thinks will work for both of them.

From our experience in our Synergistic Selling program, many salespeople would not have risked confronting the situation knowing they had the ace to fall back on if something went wrong. That is, no approved proofs. So they could be right and the client wrong. Or salespeople just lay down the law. No approved proofs, no brochure. But those win-lose approaches are not the way to build strong relationships with customers.

In addition, without the listening skills to hear and acknowledge the other's concerns, many situations such as this one blow up into a conflict where someone wins and someone loses. That's the importance of the shifting-gears technique.

I-Messages—declarative, preventive, responsive, appreciative, and confrontive—provide you a new tool to more effectively communicate and express your needs, views, and feelings. No one can read your mind. While we addressed the possible risks of authentic self-expression, the benefits are overwhelming. A whole new level of relationship—synergistic partnerships—opens up with the courage to be more honest and authentic.

Chapter Summary

1. When you are open, honest, and authentic in your communication with people, you'll feel stronger, more responsible, and confident.

2. Your past conditioning limits your self-expression.
3. Because of the possibility and consequences of upsetting the other person, you don't share what you are really thinking during a conversation.
4. When you take off your professional salesperson mask and become more authentic, you pave the way for the buyer to do the same.
5. The most effective way to communicate authentically to others is through I-Messages that are
   - declarative;
   - preventive;
   - responsive;
   - appreciative;
   - confrontive.
6. The three objectives when deciding to confront the unacceptable behavior of another person are
   - to get relief from the problem;
   - to preserve the other's self-esteem;
   - to keep the relationship intact.
7. The three parts of a Confrontive I-Message are
   - a nonjudgmental description of the unacceptable behavior;
   - the tangible effects on you;
   - your feelings about the situation.
8. After confronting another person, it may be necessary to shift gears and listen to understand their issues and concerns.

THE IMPACT OF

AUTHENTIC

COMMUNICATION

Be fair with others, but then keep after them until they're fair with you.

— *ALAN ALDA*

LaVonne is the salesperson in chapter 1 whose problems with her sales manager were affecting her performance. A salesperson with a good seven-year track record at her company, she was ready to give up and resign because of the pressure and policing practices her manager was applying. Furthermore, she was feeling inadequate and doubting her own capabilities.

During the Synergistic Selling course, she decided to take a major risk and confront the issues with her boss. She was very concerned about the possibility of making the situation worse. With coaching, over the next couple of months, she confronted him on several occasions and assertively communicated her problem. Those conversations transformed their relationship. Instead of being critical and controlling, he became very supportive and she became more open to his input. When I (Carl Zaiss) saw her at the company's national sales meeting, I was surprised at her appearance. She looked and acted happy and confident. Likewise, her performance improved. Within six months, her sales were 16 percent over budget, and by the end of the year she was the top producer in the region.

Obviously, this turnabout would not have happened on its own. It took LaVonne's courage to step out and communicate her needs to her boss to change the frustrating situation. Instead of reacting to what was going on around her, she took charge of her life.

Authentic, open, and honest communication with others is not only a valuable tool in building effective relationships; it is also personally very rewarding. The ability to speak the truth is the sign of a confident and competent salesperson.

THE UNSPOKEN CONVERSATION EXERCISE

In the previous chapter, we gave an example of the unspoken conversation exercise used in one of our courses. Participants are asked to script a conversation as they think it would go and then write in the margin what they are thinking but not saying. Using that example, this time we'll rewrite the script to reflect how the conversation might go using I-Messages to communicate what was previously unspoken.

As you may recall, Tom was having trouble with Mark, his sales support manager, not getting back to him on a timely basis.

MARK: Hello, this is Mark Johnson speaking.
TOM: Mark, it's Tom. Boy, am I glad to get you directly. I get so frustrated when I get your voice mail and have to leave a message.

MARK: I'm sorry, Tom. That new marketing program has really got us swamped around here. It seems like I'm always in a meeting.

TOM: So you guys are under a lot of pressure.

MARK: Like what else is new?

TOM: Yeah, I realize it's kind of an ongoing thing nowadays. Mark, listen, I've got a problem I want to resolve.

MARK: What's that?

TOM: I've called and left three messages for you regarding the custom design for the XYZ order. When you didn't get back to me, I got real concerned because I have a meeting with them scheduled for ten o'clock tomorrow morning.

MARK: Tom, I'm sorry, but like I told you, I'm swamped and I'm having trouble tracking down Johnson for the final approval. I'll get it taken care of by four this afternoon and fax it to you.

TOM: Once again, I hear how busy you are and that Johnson's hard to pin down. It sounds like you're running all the time just to keep your head above water.

MARK: Yeah, you got it, and I don't know how long I can keep it up.

TOM: Well, it sounds like we've got to change the system somehow if you are in meetings so much and not available to follow up on field requests. That's the reason your job was created, and I get very frustrated having to wait for you to get things done. I'm going to talk to my boss and see if we can't get you some backup. In the meantime, Mark, I just want to re-emphasize how disappointed I am when you don't return my calls.

MARK: Okay, Tom, I'm sorry. I'll get better at returning your calls and at least tell you when I don't know anything. Then, if it's a problem, we can discuss other alternatives. And I'll go find Johnson now and get back to you within the hour.

TOM: Thanks, and, Mark, I want you to know I appreciate your willingness to work on the problem. I'll see where I can help.

Quite a difference from the original conversation on page 125. Participants tell us that the experience of rewriting the conversation is very enlightening. When they communicate accurately what they are feeling with I-Messages, the other person can't help but speak more honestly, and as a result, core problems get resolved even in writing the script.

Notice in the example above that Tom uses declarative, preventive, confrontive, and appreciative I-Messages. He also listens to Mark to show that he understands Mark's view.

Authentic communication—saying what you are thinking—requires courage. This is not so much the courage to face the consequences of speaking up for yourself, but courage to overcome your past conditioning. For example, if as a child you spoke up to other friends or your family and the others teased you, laughed at you, or ignored you, you may have associated pain with "speaking your beliefs." Likewise, if you communicated your beliefs to someone by using a You-Message like "You have certainly been inconsiderate of my time," you may again have upset the other person and had to deal with their reaction. From these examples, and many others like these in your life, you formed certain beliefs. Courage is needed to overcome this conditioning.

This chapter provides you the opportunity to break out of those self-imposed limitations and become more authentic with others. We'll show you examples of authentic communication in your relationships with customers, your manager, and others essential to your success in selling. What's required from you is three commitments:

1. The first is a commitment to yourself—to tell the truth as you see it and to tell it at a deeper level than you have before. Try it. Telling the truth produces miracles in relationships.

2. The second is a commitment to your product and/or service. You've probably heard this before, but it needs reinforcing. Integrity is a vital element of

synergistic partnerships. If you are not committed
to your product or service and don't believe your
buyer will benefit, you may be a successful "peddler";
but you won't bring the integrity to the relationship
that is so essential. Not only will buyers notice
blocks to their trust issues with you, but also you
will sabotage yourself during the process.

3.   The third is a commitment to customer service. In
addition to the benefits of your product or service,
you bring value to the relationship. That value is
your commitment to satisfying your customer. That
may mean "confronting the system" in your organization.
Top-flight customer service demands that
employees take in-house risks to ensure satisfied
customers.

Determining where you stand on these commitments will
help you take the necessary actions.

One of our course participants, Jaime, expressed her frustration with one of her clients who had sent out a detailed bid
request form to be completed and returned. No personal contact, just fill out the form and send it back. Jaime works for
a travel-management firm, and personal contact is important
to their success. During our discussion on the three commitments for authentic communication, she noticed she had a
commitment to herself, to her product, and to providing her
customers personal service. On the next break, she called her
client and communicated her frustration. The result: an appointment the next week to personally review the client's
needs and therefore the opportunity for Jaime to develop a
more detailed and customized proposal for the client.

In another situation, Don, a sales representative for a
major automotive parts manufacturer, committed to being
more authentic in his relationships with others. Three days
later his commitment was tested. He received a message from
one of his clients canceling the last order and saying he was
changing product lines. Don was new to the territory, but he
had heard of the client's upsets over poor service. He picked

up the phone and told the customer no, that canceling the last order was an unacceptable solution to the problem for him and that he wanted a meeting to address the issues.

The customer was more than a little surprised at Don's stand and decided to discuss the situation. As a result, Don saved an account worth over $150,000 annually.

Real breakthroughs occur when you risk confronting others. You break through the limitations of your past conditioning and communicate authentically to others. Obstacles to productive relationships can then be removed and new possibilities opened up.

Let's explore now the three primary areas where authentic communication and I-Messages have direct application in the selling-buying process: when the other person's behavior is causing you a problem; when you are initiating the seller-buyer relationship; and when you are discussing the benefits of your products or services.

WHEN THE OTHER PERSON'S BEHAVIOR IS CAUSING YOU A PROBLEM

Let's address this point in three parts, addressing first a problem with a buyer, second a problem with an internal-support department, and finally, a problem with your sales manager.

WHEN YOU HAVE A PROBLEM WITH THE BUYER'S BEHAVIOR

A situation that frustrates many salespeople is when the buyer does not supply pertinent information needed by the seller to implement the buying decision. So let's set up this scenario to use as an example.

Moore Manufacturing recently agreed to upgrade their computerized order-entry system. They selected Hi-Tech Electronics, where the contract is being processed, and they are eager to get moving on the transition. Nancy, Hi-Tech's account executive, is frustrated with Jack, Moore's customer service manager, because he has not provided information that she needs for her people to plan the turnover time schedule. Two weeks ago during a project meeting he promised to get her the information within a week.

In this situation, Nancy's needs are not being met. She is frustrated and resentful of Jack, and yet doesn't want to upset him. To her, the situation is especially delicate since the contract is not officially signed. On the other hand, she needs the information for the project team meeting tomorrow. Without it, she's worried that Hi-Tech will fall behind in its commitments and upset the client. On the way into work this morning, she reviewed her options: (1) accept the other person's behavior, (2) change herself, or (3) attempt to influence Jack to change.

She concluded that she couldn't accept Jack's behavior and simply hope the information got to her before the meeting. She could blame the lack of information on Jack so that she'd be in the clear with her project management people, and Hi-Tech would have an excuse if Moore got upset over the time schedule. But there was too much at risk. Likewise, she didn't see a way she could change herself to resolve the issue. She did feel that some tension existed between her and Jack and didn't know what the cause was. She also considered going to Jack's boss, Marvin, but realized that was a win-lose solution that would create additional problems. So she decided to send a Confrontive I-Message to Jack in an attempt to resolve the problem. She remembered that the objectives in confronting another individual are

- to get relief from the problem, usually through a change in the customer's actions;
- to preserve the customer's self-esteem and pride;
- to keep the relationship intact, even improving it if possible.

Nancy developed a Confrontive I-Message including the three parts: (1) a nonblameful description of the other's unacceptable behavior; (2) the specific, concrete, and tangible effects on her; and (3) her feelings about the effects. She called Jack when she got to the office. The conversation went like this (notice the "shifting gears" technique that allows her to let Jack know she understands his view, too):

JACK: Good morning, Jack Barnes speaking.

NANCY: Jack, it's Nancy Taylor at Hi-Tech. I've got a problem I want to discuss with you, and I'm a little concerned about your reaction.

JACK: Oh, what's up?

NANCY: Well, Jack, I haven't received the data I need for tomorrow's project meeting that you promised last week, and I'm really concerned because we can't produce a realistic implementation schedule without it.

JACK: I'm sorry, Nancy, but this decision has created a lot of confusion over here. Many of my people don't like this vendor change, and on top of that my assistant is on vacation. It's just going to have to wait.

NANCY: Sounds like you've got a lot of challenges with this decision to upgrade your system.

JACK: You bet. We haven't even got a signed contract, and I'm being told to jam this system change into an already tight schedule. Something's got to give.

NANCY: So from your standpoint you don't understand the rush, especially with everything else going on in your department.

JACK: That's right, Nancy.

NANCY: Okay, Jack. I think I've got an understanding of the issues you are facing. My problem is that I have a project meeting tomorrow to begin the planning for your installation. Our two organizations have agreed to rush on this, and that's why we're proceeding without a contract. I need that data from you for tomorrow's meeting. If we're better organized now, it's going to save you and me a lot of headaches down the road.

JACK: Okay. If you'll come over this morning, I'll give you the information you need for tomorrow's meeting verbally. I just don't have the time to fill out the entire question-

naire you sent. A lot of that stuff is not necessary right
now.

NANCY: So the amount of detail we were asking for on the
form is a problem. Okay. I'll be over at eleven-thirty, and
we can go through what I need for the meeting.

JACK: That works for me. I'll see you then.

NANCY: And, Jack, come to think of it, either today or in the
near future, I'd like to talk with you about some of your
other concerns. It sounds like you're under a lot of pressure with this decision and you're questioning the time
schedule. Maybe it would be easier for both of us if I had
a good understanding of your concerns and the impact of
the time schedule on your department.

JACK: That sounds fine with me. It doesn't seem like anyone
around here understands. It's just "Do the job!" I'll see
you shortly.

By "taking a risk" and confronting the situation, Nancy
not only will be prepared for the meeting, but she also made
sure Jack "won." In addition, she discovered some other information that down the way may have blocked the progress on
the project. She enhanced her existing relationship with Jack
and laid the groundwork for a partnership to insure a successful implementation and create a satisfied and loyal customer.
None of this would have happened without the authentic communication from Nancy.

WHEN YOU HAVE A PROBLEM WITH AN ASSOCIATE'S BEHAVIOR

Many relationships besides the seller-buyer relationship impact one's success in selling today. This is true both in large
organizations and in smaller companies like real estate agen-
cies. Our corporate clients consistently tell us that the biggest
value of the Synergistic Selling course came from improved
internal relationships among departments. And real estate
salespeople say that the skills improve relationships with
lending institutions, title companies, and others who impact a

sale, even after the seller and buyer have agreed on the terms.

Let's now deal with situations when your problem is with someone other than your customer. For continuity, we'll just use the same situation with Jack and Nancy. Now, however, it's two months later, and Jack has just called and informed Nancy about a problem he is having with Hi-Tech's customer-support training department. It seems that they are always changing the dates of training at the last minute, and this morning an instructor showed up on the wrong day. Jack has talked to Ralph, the department's manager, but nothing seems to change. So the problem now lands in Nancy's lap.

As she looks at the issue, she realizes the natural instinct is to go to her boss and get him to lean on Ralph to handle her client better. After all, she has an upset client, and "customer service" is a good tool to use in beating on someone. That would guarantee her that Jack would get taken care of. Or would it? She then remembers the consequences of that win-lose approach. Specifically, losers resent winners, and Ralph's resentment could manifest itself in many different forms. At best, all she would get from Ralph is compliance—he would do only what's necessary in a begrudging sort of way to make Jack happy. Nothing more, and no commitment to improve customer satisfaction in general.

Likewise, she isn't willing to let it go, even though again there is some risk. The relationship with Ralph's department is critical to her. She needs his support. Ralph has been with the company a long time and has developed a very powerful "empire." The technical nature of Hi-Tech's product demands a great deal of customer-support training, and Ralph has a very strong and technically proficient staff. Upper management has a strong technical orientation and pretty much lets Ralph do his own thing. After all, by the time customers get to Ralph, the contract is signed. Sales has done their job; now it is up to Ralph's department to train the customer's people. Ralph is, in fact, one of those sacred cows you can find in every organization.

Out of her personal commitment to customer satisfaction

and her commitment to Jack, she decides it is time to send Ralph a Confrontive I-Message:

RALPH: Ralph McGuire speaking.

NANCY: Good morning, Ralph, it's Nancy Taylor.

RALPH: Yes, Nancy, what can I do for you?

NANCY: Ralph, when you make last-minute changes in the training schedule at Moore, Jack gets upset. He just called me, and now I have to spend time tracking down the situation. That frustrates me. I'm also concerned about the interruptions in an already difficult time schedule.

RALPH: Okay, Nancy, I'll take care of it.

NANCY: Just hearing you say you'll take care of it doesn't work for me, Ralph. I'd like to know what's going on at Moore.

RALPH: Look, we're swamped with last-minute requests from the installation at the university, and because of the politics, that's the priority. So we're doing the best we can until that project is over.

NANCY: So what you're saying is that the problems at the university are causing a lot of last-minute changes in our other accounts.

RALPH: You got it!

NANCY: I don't like that at all. We've spent a lot of time on the Moore installation because of the time pressures, and I'm not comfortable with problems with another client interfering and causing problems. That doesn't make sense to me, yet I can understand how it must put you in the middle.

RALPH: I don't mind that. It's been that way around here for years. Everything's a priority until something more important comes up. Don't worry about it. It all works out.

NANCY: So, from your view, it's just something we have to live with and make the best of. And reading between the lines, I hear you telling me not to make a big deal out of it: "Don't make waves."

RALPH: You do what you've got to do. I'm just saying until

the university project is complete, we'll have to be flexible over at Moore.

NANCY: Well, that gets our needs met, but not Jack's. Last-minute changes over there cause him a lot of problems. He's short-staffed now, and scheduling people for your training classes is a major chore. Then when they get changed, he goes through the roof. And talk about politics, their president plays tennis with Bob [Hi-Tech's president]. That's why we're there and why we started without a contract. I don't want this problem to get to that level and get Bob involved. I think I understand your problem, and what I want is for you and me to have a session with Jack to hear his problem. Maybe we can work together to look at some other solutions. Will you go with me to meet with Jack?

RALPH: Okay. Set up the meeting and let my secretary know. But I'm not sure it will do any good.

NANCY: Yeah, I hear your doubts. And, Ralph, thanks for taking the time and working with me on this. I appreciate it. I also would like to get some input from you on how I can go about improving our overall commitment to customer service.

As a result, Nancy not only has taken a major step in getting Moore's problem solved but has also opened the door to an improved relationship with Ralph and established a dialogue with a critical support department.

Businesses and other organizations spend millions of dollars annually on customer-service training. Most of it is spent on "smile" or "courtesy" training for those employees who have customer contact. Real customer service comes from the very bowels of an organization. Most organizations don't cultivate the environment that allows people like Nancy to feel comfortable in changing the system. They feel like a salmon swimming upstream—alone.

It is surprising to hear story after story about breakdowns in customer service that result from problems in relationships within an organization, problems that are easily resolved when individuals take risks, break through the limitations of the existing culture, and are authentic in their communications with each other. In the example above, Nancy did just that in attempting to get her problem solved.

WHEN YOU HAVE A PROBLEM WITH YOUR SALES MANAGER

Perhaps the most difficult individual to confront is your boss. For many salespeople there is a great deal of fear surrounding authority figures in their lives. Salespeople fear repercussions and reprisals. In addition, they worry that upsetting their boss may cost them their job, the next promotion, or, at the very least, negative comments on the next performance evaluation. Others are concerned that they may be labeled as troublemakers.

Ironically, these fears are prevalent at all levels of the organization. Recently, I (Carl Zaiss) contracted to deliver Synergistic Selling to the field sales staff of a Fortune 500 manufacturing company. The first few courses were conducted for the first-level salespeople, the district managers. When I got to this portion of the course, the participants rebelled, claiming that there was no way they could confront their bosses, the zone managers. After all, zone managers were dictatorial and were not open to this kind of honest communication. By the time they finished describing their managers, I was convinced that zone managers in this company were monsters who walked around with eyes in the middle of their foreheads and blood dripping from their fangs.

Then I was asked to deliver the program to the zone managers, and to my surprise they looked and acted like normal human beings. When I again got to the part of the course on confronting your boss, they reacted and described their bosses, the regional managers, in the same way the district managers had described them. From their description, I again walked away with this picture of regional managers being monsters with eyes in the middle of their foreheads and blood dripping from their fangs. Not a pretty picture. When I met with the regional managers, I found again normal human beings just trying to do their job the best way they knew how. And they reacted the same way when I talked about confronting their bosses, the area managers. Furthermore, the area managers voiced the same concern about confronting the vice president of sales.

The fear of confronting one's boss is a human condition not restricted to one particular organization, one particular industry, or one particular country. The fear of authority figures is the result of our growing up in a win-lose culture. If you don't think this applies to you, just stop and look hard at the feelings that come over you when you see the lights of a police car in your rearview mirror. Whether guilty or not, most people feel fear.

For an example of confronting a sales manager, let's return to Howard's situation as mentioned in chapter 1. Howard, the salesperson for the automotive financing company, is irritated that his boss continues to pull him into the credit department to help cover when they get behind. This results in Howard's having to constantly change his schedule. Notice in this dialogue how he shifts gears and listens to the branch manager's problems also.

HOWARD (1): Linda, do you have a moment? I've got a problem I want to discuss with you.

LINDA: Sure, Howard, what's up?

HOWARD (2): Thanks, I'm actually a little nervous bringing this up, but it's becoming a major issue for me, and I want to get it resolved. The problem is, Linda, that when you pull me off of my sales function to cover in the credit department, I get upset because I have to change my schedule. Yesterday, I even had to cancel a meeting with the finance manager over at Don Scott's new dealership.

LINDA: I understand it's an inconvenience for you, Howard, but we have a priority to take care of dealers. In this economy, they don't want to risk missing a single sale due to a slowdown in getting finance requests processed. So I'm afraid there's nothing we can do about it.

HOWARD (3): So you're saying that because of the heat we get from slow processing of credit applications, that's got to be our priority, right?

LINDA: That's right, Howard. And anyway, when Mary gets bogged down in there, I expect people to be willing to jump in and help. That's what teamwork is all about.

HOWARD (4): You sound pretty committed to that.

LINDA: Yeah, I am. Is that a problem for you?

HOWARD (5): Look, I don't have any problem with the commitment to teamwork. My problem is that I don't like being pulled off of my responsibilities at the last minute and having to change my schedule. It's uncomfortable for me to be yanked around like that, and besides I look like an idiot to my clients.

LINDA: Well, I'm sorry about that. It's just that you know the department so well and you're the only one I can count on.

HOWARD (6): I got that, Linda. Mary gets swamped with financing requests, and because of our commitment to improve our processing times for the dealers, you've got to react with the quickest solution you can, and I'm it if I'm here.

LINDA: That's it on the button, Howard. Sorry.

HOWARD (7): Okay, but that doesn't work for me. First of all, it sends a message to the staff that the sales function isn't that important. Second, it affects my credibility with the dealers, and finally, I don't like working in a crisis situation where I'm always putting out fires and can't get my job done. I'm worried that in a few months you and Tom [the regional sales manager] will get on me about our sales volume, and I'll bet the team won't be there to make calls with me. I believe in teamwork, but I think we all have our individual responsibilities to the team also. Mine is to bring in sales, not play financial clerk in the credit office.

LINDA: So this is really a problem for you, isn't it?

HOWARD (8): Yeah, it is. It's really bothering me.

LINDA: Okay, have you got any ideas?

HOWARD (9): Yes, I do. But what I'd like to suggest is that

you, Mary, and me get together and look at the problem. I want to get Mary involved since it affects her area. Maybe by putting our heads together, we can come up with something that works for everyone.

LINDA: Okay, talk to Mary and set it up for Friday after lunch.

HOWARD (10): Fine, and Linda, thanks for being open to other options. I appreciate it that we can talk frankly like this.

Howard sets the stage for this conversation very effectively by communicating his feelings and then delivering a good Confrontive I-Message in #2. He then shifts gears in responses #3 and #4 and listens to Linda to make sure she knows he understood her. In #5 he reasserts his initial problem, and in #6 he summarizes her full position. When he knows that she feels that she's been totally understood, it's then easier to present the total picture for her as he does in #7, rather than blasting her with it right away. By then he has demonstrated his willingness to listen and understand her views. And in #9, they agree to have a meeting with Mary to resolve the issue. That meeting will utilize the six-step process for no-lose conflict resolution addressed in the next chapter.

You have a responsibility to confront your manager when things aren't working for you. It's the only way to free yourself from obstacles blocking your success. Your choice is to take things as they are and play the victim role, resenting your boss, yourself, and even others around you; or to accept the responsibility for your own life and success as a salesperson. Empower yourself and be willing to use this tool in even the most difficult of situations. You'll find this form of honest self-expression very rewarding.

Effective confrontation is an essential tool in building productive, synergistic, and mutually rewarding relationships with others. It's the only way to resolve your problems with buyers, others who impact the selling process, and your manager in a way that both parties win—no one loses. This is a fundamental principle in the Synergistic Paradigm.

INITIATING THE SELLER-BUYER RELATIONSHIP

The seller-buyer relationship may be initiated by either person. When the buyer initiates the process, she begins by saying something to the effect of "I need something you might have." This is most obvious in the retail sales environment. The seller initiates the process with a message that implies, "I have something you might need."

When a salesperson initiates a relationship, an authentic I-Message is often helpful. In this case, the seller has to be prepared to convey a message that has a high probability of sparking the interest of the buyer. In the sentence "I have something you might need," the most important portion is "you might need." Many salespeople in the marketplace focus on what they are selling, but the buyer wants to hear what's in it for them. And the most important word in the sentence is "might." This implies that the seller doesn't really know if the buyer could use the product or service until they look at the buyer's individual needs. In this way salespeople avoid the typical buyer resistance found in the sales arrogance of most opening statements.

Here are some of the strongest door openers or messages that salespeople can use to increase the probability of a buyer's agreeing to begin a relationship.

1. *Messages about the possibilities of saving money:*
   "I have some information on our new loan package that might save you some money in refinancing your home."
   "I have some information on our new accounting software that might save you some money in payroll preparation."
2. *Messages about a new product or service and its benefits:*
   "I'd like to tell you about our new surgical gown that might reduce your uniform replacement expense."
   "I'd like to share some information with you about our new 800 service which might help you market your services."

3. *Messages that imply the product or service will help the buyer do her job better:*
   "I'd like to discuss our sales training program and how it might improve the performance of your people in the field."
   "I have some information on our personal computer system that you might find will save you time in accessing vendor files."
4. *Messages that say the seller has new information for the buyer:*
   "I have some new information on our system that might save your people some time in researching questions."
   "I'd like to review this new product information as it might help you train your people more effectively."
5. *Messages that imply solving a problem the buyer has:*
   "I have a new cleaning product that might solve that carpet problem you have in the reception area."
   "I'd like to review our new color printing process that might give you more flexibility in developing your promotional materials."

As you can see, each of the above messages promises the buyer some benefit. By delivering that benefit message in the "I have something you might need" form, you will greatly enhance the impact on the buyer.

DISCUSSING THE BENEFITS OF YOUR PRODUCT OR SERVICE

Most salespeople know the difference between a feature and a benefit, and yet it's amazing how much time salespeople spend talking about the features of their product or service. Certainly, customers do need to know how the product is made and what features it contains, but they do not appreciate it based only on that information. Value is created from the buyer's perception of what the product or service will do for them—the benefit.

A feature is anything that describes the product or service. Features are often expressed as nouns. A feature is a physical characteristic that answers the question "What is it?" Each feature tells something about the product or service. A feature of a new car is the passenger-side air bag. The benefit of each feature is a personalized value that answers the question "What does that mean to me?" The new car buyer needs to hear, "The passenger-side air bag makes this car as safe for your spouse and children as it is for you." So everyone probably agrees that saying "This car has a passenger-side air bag, which makes the car as safe for your passengers as it is for you" is much better than saying "This car has a passenger-side air bag."

Now let's take it a step deeper to enhance the impact of the benefit statement. Read the following statements out loud:

1. This car has a passenger-side air bag, which makes the car as safe for your passenger as it is for you.
2. You'll really like the passenger-side air bag, which makes it as safe for your passenger as it is for you.
3. We designed this car with a passenger-side air bag, which makes this car as safe for your passenger as it is for you.
4. I think you'll like the addition of the passenger-side air bag, which makes this car as safe for your passenger as it is for you.

Statement 1 is a generic sentence with minimal impact. It's okay in general advertising, but it doesn't build a personal bridge between individuals. The second statement is a You-Message and may create resistance to the statement. Many people, when told what they should do or feel, automatically think, "You wanna bet?" The third statement uses the generality of "we." In the example, "we" is the giant, impersonal automobile company. It is vague and doesn't grab the buyer.

Example 4 is an I-Message and personalizes the impact of the benefit. Remember, your customers are buying from you, and the relationship you have with them is an essential element in the sales process. As with other authentic communication, the benefit delivered with an I-Message enables the buyer to see the salesperson as a real person with her own thoughts and feelings and not a robot delivering a carefully prepared presentation.

Here's another example:

1. Our health club has over thirty pieces of cardiovascular equipment, which means you won't have to wait in line as often.
2. You'll really like the fact that we have over thirty pieces of cardiovascular equipment, which means you won't have to wait in line as often.
3. We designed this club with over thirty pieces of cardiovascular equipment so you won't have to wait in line as often.
4. I think you'll appreciate the fact that we have over thirty pieces of cardiovascular equipment, which means you won't have to wait in line as often.

Again, notice how much more personal the fourth example sounds. A little change with big impact.

Buyers want to work with salespeople they can trust. Authentic communication is essential in building that trust. In addition, you'll be happier and more successful in your selling role when you are more natural and genuine and when you get your needs met. Take a risk, take off your professional-salesperson mask, and let the natural and unique person inside you emerge. You'll be pleasantly surprised at the results.

Chapter Summary

1. To authentically communicate with others is to take responsibility for your own life and results in greater pride, confidence, and personal effectiveness.
2. I-Messages make it easier to speak what is typically unspoken during a conversation as they minimize the risk of upsetting the other person.
3. The three primary areas where authentic communication and I-Messages have direct application in the selling-buying process are
   - when the customer's (or another person's) behavior is causing you a problem;
   - when you are initiating the selling-buying process;
   - when you are discussing the benefits of your product or service.
4. One of the keys to effective customer satisfaction is the willingness of individuals within the organization to confront each other and eliminate operational obstacles.
5. The best way to initiate the selling-buying process is to construct and deliver an I-Message around the sentence "I have something you might need."
6. The use of "I" language greatly enhances the impact of messages about the benefits of your product or service.

HOW TO RESOLVE
CONFLICTS SO THAT
NO ONE LOSES

Instead of denying conflict, this is an invitation to embrace it and understand it. When we do, it becomes one of the greatest gifts we have for positive growth and change, an empowering and energizing opportunity.

—THOMAS CRUM

George is a field sales engineer for a high-tech manufacturer of custom-built integrated circuits. Ninety-five percent of his business comes from one customer. Delivery times normally range between six to twelve weeks; however, on one special occasion, they were able to manufacture and deliver a product in four weeks. Now the purchasing manager thinks that if he applies enough pressure, he can get a four-week delivery on all orders. He consistently makes threatening comments such as "We're not going to use you anymore" or "You'd better shorten your delivery time or we'll find someone who will work with us."

George has good relationships with other members of this client organization, especially the engineers he works with on the product design. He is also aware that there is a great deal more business potential, so it bothers him that the conflict with the purchasing manager is resulting in lower sales volume than he would like.

No one has the courage to confront the situation. George does not want to make an already difficult problem worse. The engineers and others within the client organization would like to do more business with George's company, but they won't do anything about the problem because of the power the purchasing manager has in their organization. And George's sales manager is afraid of losing the sales they do have. So nothing happens.

Out of their fear of conflict, everyone is in a silent conspiracy with everyone else: they'll accept the situation just as it is. You can just hear them saying, "That's just the way it is around here" or "Do the best job you can under the circumstances." The purchasing manager will never change, and there's no way to get around him. Then each participant makes up a story that works for him as to why the situation is the way it is. This is their way of rationalizing what's going on and why they can't do anything about it.

For example, George blames the internal departments in his organization, criticizing them for everything that goes wrong. This approach damages internal support for George's client, since the support departments must defend themselves. The easiest way to do that is blame other factors, like the client for poor input, or the sales department for the way the information is processed, or a current "tighten the belt" directive for the fact that they are shortstaffed and overworked. The result is a lot of meetings on these problems and issues. The frustration level then increases because the meetings take a great deal of time and the real issues never get discussed.

The conspiracy is maintained within the client organization as well. The engineers and others who would like to do more work with George's company escape their responsibility by reminding themselves, "Everyone here knows you don't question the purchasing manager's authority. After all, he has been with the company for twenty-five years, and he's often acknowledged by the president for his tough negotiating with suppliers. And anyway, everyone knows that creating competition between suppliers is the best way to improve quality and service and reduce cost." So the supporters of George's company choose not to rock the boat.

As a result, the partnership with the supplier that would foster creativity and innovation, and reduce costs, cannot be built. This kind of relationship would allow George's company to be more involved in the long-range planning and, therefore, project future needs more effectively.

Sadly, the purchasing manager, who is committed to doing a good job for his company, is working in the dark and is never given the opportunity to examine new options. No one has the courage to speak up and allow the purchasing manager to understand the consequences of his behavior. He goes on his merry way unaware of the problems he is creating and thinking he is doing a good job for his company.

All this occurs out of the fear of confronting others and not dealing with the conflicts openly and honestly. Situations of this nature run rampant throughout today's organizations, and the consequences dramatically impact sales, customer satisfaction, and profitability.

Everyone in sales has experienced conflicts at times— they are a part of the business, a part of life, for that matter. Differences of opinion and disagreements can't be avoided. Most people actually fear conflict as a result of growing up in a culture founded on the principles of the traditional win-lose paradigm. Typically, most individuals have experienced conflict as an argument or fight where someone wins and someone loses. We all know too well the hurt feelings and emotions associated with the injured and broken relationships resulting from conflicts.

The fear of conflict takes different forms. People fear

damaging a relationship that has existed for some time; they fear repercussions or reprisals from others; and they worry about upsetting the other person. Many fear looking foolish or self-centered, and still others fear being ostracized by the team as a result of their "negative attitude."

Therefore, conflict is often seen as a disease that must be eradicated or avoided at all costs. People then employ one of two strategies: the "ostrich approach"—avoid it, don't admit it exists, don't talk about the differences and disagreements—or the "I'll do anything to keep peace in the family approach." These two approaches have serious consequences for salespeople and their relationships with their buyers, their support departments, and their managers.

The conventional thinking and behaviors surrounding conflict are primitive at best, and ineffective in today's complex marketplace. A new approach to conflict and the necessary skills is critical as the network of individuals involved in the sales process expands, and the trend toward long-term relationships with customers grows.

In the Synergistic Paradigm, conflict is seen as an opportunity to remove an obstacle and improve the relationship. You have to believe this! It really is possible to resolve a conflict so that no one loses and both parties win. There are three guidelines to effective no-lose conflict resolution in the Synergistic Paradigm. First, accept conflicts as a normal part of all relationships. Second, commit yourself to no-lose (or win-win) conflict resolutions. Third, use the six-step method presented in this chapter for finding mutually acceptable solutions. These guidelines are the keys to becoming more comfortable with conflicts and more effective at resolving them. Let's examine each in greater detail.

ACCEPT CONFLICT AS A NORMAL PART
OF ALL RELATIONSHIPS

Conflicts are inevitable and serve a healthy function in every relationship. In fact, the absence of conflict may mean one party is intimidated by the other—salesperson afraid to confront a customer, subordinate afraid to challenge a supervisor. The key is not to avoid or deny conflicts but to learn how to approach and resolve them in a way that actually benefits the relationship. The fact that you feel in conflict with another person signals that something is not right in the relationship. Thus, through conflict you can improve the relationship and stimulate creative thinking that may bring you higher levels of satisfaction from the relationship.

To accept conflict as a normal, and even healthy, part of a relationship requires that you look at how you feel about conflict based on your past experiences. Rather than being the victim of this past conditioning, try to feel that you are free to acquire new skills for resolving conflicts. A man in one of our training sessions explained it this way:

> I remember, while growing up, that anytime I had a problem with another person my mother would tell me, don't stoop to their level. This was obviously her way of teaching me to be a mature person who doesn't get into fights. Nice people didn't get in conflicts. Only recently have I seen the impact these beliefs have had on my life. Rather than confronting issues causing conflict with others, I habitually would duck the issue and withdraw from the relationship.
>
> Throughout my life I have avoided conflict with other people and compounded the problem by being arrogant (not stooping to their level) about it. As a result, I came across as aloof and distant, and the other person would then avoid me. It was not a healthy way to build relationships. When I did get hooked into a conflict, I was very disgusted with myself.

Most people have experienced similar conditioning and believe that conflict is wrong. They then go to great lengths to avoid or deny the conflicts in their lives. The consequences:

problems don't get resolved; resentment builds in the relationship until it erupts out of proportion to the particular problem at the moment; and relationships remain tense and uncomfortable, thereby blocking effective communication.

Furthermore, salespeople want to be liked, and therefore, most don't address the conflicts with their customers. Again, from their conditioning, they equate getting into a conflict with their customer with their customer's not liking them. As a result, they wear a phony smile to signify that everything is okay, while inside they resent their customer, their job, and themselves.

The point is, you have to look at your own history with conflict. If you take the time to identify these limiting beliefs, you'll become more effective in resolving your problems with buyers and others in your life. Break out of your past conditioning and accept conflicts as an opportunity to improve the relationship. If you perceive conflict as something of value, you will be more likely to understand it, more comfortable with it, and more committed to addressing and resolving it.

COMMIT YOURSELF TO NO-LOSE (OR WIN-WIN) CONFLICT RESOLUTIONS

There are three basic methods of resolving conflict. The first two represent the traditional win-lose paradigm, and the third, the no-lose, Synergistic Paradigm.

METHOD 1: YOU WIN, OTHER LOSES

This problem-solving approach is rooted in the use of power to impose a solution on another. the person using Method 1 essentially says: "I have the most power in our relationship in the form of rewards and punishments, so I will win." The person with less power generally takes this position: "I reluctantly accept your solution, but I resent your using power on me, and I'll find some way of getting back the first chance I get."

Following are some examples of the Method 1 approach to resolving conflicts:

- Tom, a salesperson for a medical products company, and his distributor are in a disagreement over a new merchandising program. The distributor is upset that he was not involved in the design of the new program and questions its effectiveness. Tom informs him that he has no choice as the home office has already developed the materials, and the costs will be charged against the distributor's marketing fee. Tom and his company win and the distributor loses.
- Mary, an advertising account executive with a magazine publisher, requests extra help from her layout department to pull together a last-minute ad for one of her new customers. Mike, the manager of the layout department, says he can't do it as they are under pressure to meet another deadline. Mary goes over Mike's head to his boss with the promise that this new customer means a lot of business potential for the company. Mike is told to work his staff on the weekend to get it done. Mary wins and Mike loses.
- Anthony, the regional sales manager for a large software manufacturer, asks one of his sales reps, Kelly, to be available to meet with the vice president of sales, who is in town for an inspection trip. Kelly has two presentations scheduled and prefers not to change her appointments. Anthony, wanting Kelly to be involved in the meeting with his boss, orders her to change her schedule. Anthony wins and Kelly loses.

METHOD 2: OTHER WINS, YOU LOSE

In the permissive conflict-resolution approach, one person yields to the demands of another rather than stand up for his needs. He lets the other person win for a number of reasons: fear of losing the relationship, dislike of emotional conflict, desire to be a good guy, and so on.

Here are some examples of the Method 2 approach to resolving conflict:

- Sandra, a salesperson with a business-forms supply company, and her client, Dennis, have a problem. Dennis approved the layout of a new form, and now that they have been printed, his boss is refusing to accept them. To cover himself with his boss, Dennis threatens to take all of their future business to a competitor unless Sandra reprints the order at no charge. To keep the business, Sandra reluctantly agrees to Dennis's demands. Sandra loses and Dennis wins.
- Darryl, an account executive with a major training firm, has a client who has requested that his company prepare customized workbooks for the leadership-training program they purchased from him. He goes to Steven, the director of program development, with his client's request and is told that they don't have the time to customize the training materials. Darryl loses and Steven wins.
- Betty, a salesperson at an automotive dealership, is asked by her manager to come in on her days off this week to cover the floor. She replies that she has already promised her children to spend some time with them. However, she agrees to change her schedule when her boss questions her attitude and her commitment to her job. Betty loses and her boss wins.

METHOD 3: YOU WIN, OTHER WINS (NO-LOSE)

Both Methods 1 and 2 leave one party a resentful loser with unmet needs. The consequences of this resentment were examined in chapter 1 and are at the very core of the limitations of the Traditional Paradigm. Method 3 is based on a totally different set of assumptions, a different paradigm, than the power-based method. The needs of both individuals are considered of equal importance. Each party, whether power is equal or unequal, is concerned about the needs of the other, as if saying, "Let's work together for a solution that meets your needs and meets my needs. Both of us will win; no one will be a resentful loser."

The main advantage of Method 3 is that it does not harm the relationship and, in fact, usually improves it. Feelings of resentment and unfairness are eliminated and replaced by mutual respect and concern for the needs of both individuals, and there are other important benefits of Method 3.

RELATIONSHIPS BECOME HEALTHIER AND MORE PRODUCTIVE

Salespeople who feel more comfortable with conflict stop avoiding it. Issues that lie below the surface of relationships with customers, managers, and others are brought to the surface and resolved in constructive ways. This eliminates many of the obstacles to sales success. Relationships with customers are built on a foundation of mutual trust and characterized by more open and honest communication.

In the critical relationships with sales managers and other support functions, core issues get resolved rather than constantly "putting out fires," blaming each other, and keeping hidden agendas. The salesperson then leads a team of people who collaborate with each other and provide superior customer service. When problems do arise, they trust each other to work through the conflict and reach a decision that satisfies everyone, including the customer.

AN INCREASED COMMITMENT TO CARRY OUT THE DECISION

Everyone has had the experience of feeling a strong commitment to carry out a decision because of having had the chance to participate in the decision-making process. With this chance to participate comes ownership for the solution rather than the resistance created by someone unilaterally making the decision and forcing it upon us. When individuals are responsible for shaping the decision, they also feel responsible for seeing that it works.

DECISIONS ARE OFTEN OF A HIGHER QUALITY

Method 3 enlists the creativity, experience, and brainpower of everyone involved in a conflict. Whether it be with your customer, your manager, or others involved in your selling process, the thought that "two heads are better than one" makes particularly good sense because the needs of all parties must be represented. One person does not have the same perspective of the problem as the other and cannot even assume he knows the other's needs. Therefore, unilateral decision making limits the quality of the decisions.

DECISIONS ARE OFTEN MADE MORE QUICKLY

Most salespeople have experienced getting into a conflict with a customer or someone else that goes unresolved for weeks or months because they couldn't think of a solution. Then, after the salesperson summons the courage to approach the person, together they reached an amicable solution in minutes. Method 3 helps people in conflict get their needs and feelings out in the open, honestly face the issues, and explore possible solutions quickly. Furthermore, this method helps bring to the surface a lot of information unavailable to any of the parties operating separately, thereby making it easier to come to a quicker decision.

Method 3 requires both a commitment to no-lose conflict resolution and knowledge of the six-step method of resolving conflicts.

THE SIX-STEP METHOD FOR FINDING
MUTUALLY ACCEPTABLE SOLUTIONS

The win-win, or no-lose, method is more than an attitude or philosophy of problem solving; it's a systematic set of six steps that lead to a mutually acceptable solution to conflicts.

STEP 1: DEFINE THE PROBLEM (IN TERMS OF NEEDS,
NOT COMPETING SOLUTIONS)

This is the most critical step in conflict resolution. Your statement of the problem should not communicate blame or judgment. Sending I-Messages is the most effective way to
express your needs. After you have stated your needs and
feelings, try to verbalize your understanding of the other person's needs. If you don't know her view of the conflict, ask. Be
sure to use your active listening skills so that she knows
you've understood her views.

The key to making the six steps work is understanding
the difference between needs and solutions. So often people
get into conflicts simply because they fail to communicate
their underlying needs to each other. Instead, each sets out on
a course of action (their solution) to meet their needs. If the
solutions prove to be incompatible, a conflict emerges.

Conflicts are more easily resolved when the needs are
identified. To allow this to happen, you must let go of the position you are defending, since it is probably your solution to
the conflict and not an accurate expression of your needs. By
protecting your position and "being right," you may be limiting other options that may satisfy both your needs and those
of the other person. Needs can be identified by asking the
question "What would that do for you?" about a specific solution. For example, here's a conflict between Ann, a sales
training manager, and Mark, her vice president of sales. Ann
wanted a meeting every Friday morning to review the week's
activities, and Mark didn't want to be pinned down to a specific time. She called him unsupportive, and he thought she
was too demanding. The unresolved conflict affected their relationship, their communication, and their effectiveness.

Not until each was asked "What would that do for you?"
did they discover their true needs. Ann needed to have some
ongoing feedback about her performance and to feel included
in what was going on, and having a Friday morning meeting
was her solution to meeting those needs. Mark, on the other
hand, needed to avoid scheduling any more meetings during

the day so that he could be more available to the field sales force. Once those needs were on thc table, they decided to meet for breakfast before work one morning a week. That solution was perfectly acceptable to both.

People go to great lengths to prove they are right in a conflict, and like horses wearing blinders, they can't see other options. Many salespeople admit protecting a certain solution in a conflict when in fact they can think of a different option that works as well. The problem is, they have invested so much effort in defending their position that they don't want to appear foolish or wrong by backing away from it.

Remember the childhood story about the blind men studying the elephant? When asked to describe an elephant, the blind man with his arms around a leg said, "An elephant is like a tree trunk." Another, holding on to the elephant's trunk, said. "The elephant is like a snake." And still another, feeling the elephant's broad side, said, "No, you're both wrong. An elephant is large like the side of a barn." The question is, "Who is right and who is wrong?"

Actually, all were right from their unique perspective, and all were wrong from the other perspectives. Many of our conflicts are like that. Within an organization, each person or department has a limited view of the overall situation, yet they defend their position as if it's the only one. CEOs do that too. Yet, because of the fear of presenting differing views within an organization, many CEOs have a very limited perception. This results in many critical decisions being made in the dark.

When both parties are protecting their particular solution in a conflict, a seemingly unresolvable situation develops. This is where most people "compromise." As a result, neither party is happy, and the resentment still exists in the relationship. No-lose conflict resolution is not a compromise. Compromises occur when the parties begin modifying the conflicting solutions and come up with a solution that is begrudgingly acceptable to each. Each feels as if they've lost something.

Essential for no-lose conflict resolution is the ability to let go of "being right," setting aside the conflicting solutions, identifying the needs of each and searching for other solutions that will satisfy both individuals. This means focusing on the needs first and solutions second.

Before moving to Step 2, be sure both of you accept the definition of the problem. You can even test this out by asking the other person to accept, or reject, a statement of the problem both of you are going to resolve. Finally, make sure the other person understands clearly that you are looking for a solution that will meet both of your needs—so that neither of you will lose.

STEP 2: GENERATE POSSIBLE SOLUTIONS

This is the creative part of conflict resolution. Frequently, it is hard to come up with a good solution right away, but the initial solutions will nearly always stimulate better ones. First, ask the other person for possible solutions, then offer yours.

Try to get a large number of possible solutions before evaluating or discussing any particular one. At all costs, avoid evaluating and criticizing the other person's solutions as this stifles the creative process. Instead, write down all solutions for later review.

When you have generated a number of reasonably feasible solutions, or no other solutions can be generated, it is time to move on to Step 3.

STEP 3: EVALUATE THE SOLUTIONS

This is the stage of conflict resolution when both of you have to do some serious critical thinking. Are there any flaws in the solutions being offered? Is there any reason why a solution will not work? Will it be too hard to implement or carry out? It is important here to remember the importance of authenticity. Look inside and express your honest feelings.

STEP 4: DECIDE ON A MUTUALLY ACCEPTABLE SOLUTION

A mutual commitment to one, or a combination, of solutions must be made. This is not a compromise. A compromise is "half I win and half I lose" and "half you win and half you lose." As we said earlier, a compromise usually comes out of being stuck on one solution and then modifying it. Stay committed to finding a solution that satisfies both individuals. Usually when all the facts get exposed, the choice of a preferred solution becomes clear.

Don't make the mistake of trying to push or persuade the other person. First of all, you will create more resistance to your idea, and second, if the other person doesn't freely choose a solution that is acceptable, chances are it will not be carried out.

When it appears that you are close to a decision, state the solution to make sure you both understand it.

STEP 5: IMPLEMENT THE SOLUTION

Creating a solution, of course, does not guarantee that you can carry it out. Immediately after a solution has been agreed upon, you need to talk about implementation—*who* does *what* by *when*. The most constructive attitude is to trust that both of you will carry out the decision, rather than raise the question of the consequences if you don't.

STEP 6: EVALUATE THE RESULTS

The first solution from this no-lose process may not turn out to be the best. Sometimes, as the solution is implemented, you or the other person may discover weaknesses that need modification or even decide to reject it in favor of a better solution. Make sure you seek out the other person's feelings about the results as well as expressing your own.

Now let's go back to George's conflict with his customer, which we described at the beginning of this chapter. John, the purchasing manager that he deals with, represents 95 percent of his business, and yet George knows he can do more business with John's company and provide better service at the same time. John's constant pressure and threats keep George and others on the defensive and are a consistent source of frustration. Together they are playing the traditional win-lose game to see who can stay in control. To this point no one has wanted to confront the situation out of the fear of upsetting John and losing the $6 million in revenue that they receive now.

George finally decides that something must change as he realizes that he is carrying a great deal of resentment toward John. Because of the size of John's account, they talk almost daily, and George leaves each conversation feeling beaten up. The pressure and threats from John are taking their toll as George feels he is working under an axe that is about to fall. His resentment manifests itself in many ways. For one thing, it seems he is always upset with the internal departments that design, manufacture, and ship the integrated circuits to John's company, and the more John complains, the more upset and vocal George gets. There is a great deal of tension between him and the operational departments. In addition, George is frustrated with his boss for not stepping in and solving the problem. In private conversations, he calls his boss "weak" and "spineless." He simply does not enjoy going to work anymore.

Furthermore, his discontent at work is affecting his home life. He is always tired, and his wife is talking more about his "moods" and his "irritability." And finally, he is questioning his own abilities and self-worth. So far he has been unable to resolve the issue with John, and the constant complaining combined with the strained relationships within the company are causing him to doubt himself. This amplifies and perpetuates the problem. The consequences that George is experiencing are common occurrences for salespeople who deny or avoid conflicts, or deal with them from a win-lose posture. Remember, when you don't get your needs met in a relationship with another person, the resulting resentment manifests itself in many ways—including, but not described here, your health.

So George looked at his options. He could (1) continue to accept John's behavior, (2) change himself, or (3) attempt to influence John to change. He chose option 3 and called John to set up a meeting. Here's how that meeting might happen using the listening and authentic communication skills with the six steps of Method 3 conflict resolution.

GEORGE: John, thanks for setting aside the time to meet with me today. I think it's about time that you and I had a heart-to-heart. There's some issues between us that I would like to get resolved, and I want you to know that I'm committed to finding some ways we can build this relationship so that it works for both of us and our organizations.

JOHN: George, what issues are you talking about?

GEORGE: Well, John, when you constantly threaten to pull your business and take it elsewhere, I get concerned because it is affecting our ability to deliver the quality you want and it's costing you money.

Notice that in the first message George set the stage by communicating his commitment to resolve the issues so that both parties win. Now he'll have to model that commitment. Then, in the second message, he delivers a three-part Confrontive I-Message. Next, he's going to have to shift gears and listen to John.

JOHN: Look, who do you think you are? If it wasn't for my staying on you guys, I doubt that you'd ever do anything right! You're just not dependable unless someone's looking over your shoulder.

GEORGE: So you're convinced that nothing would happen without constantly kicking us in the rear.

JOHN: That's right and hear this. We give you guys six million dollars a year in business and you think we're married to you. If I didn't stay on top of things, you'd take shortcuts every chance you get and stick it to us when we're not looking. Anyway, that's my job: to keep you guys and others like you in line.

GEORGE: So you're worried that we'd take advantage of the situation, and you see that your job is to make sure we don't.

JOHN: That's right!

GEORGE: And besides that, you think all suppliers should be treated like that.

JOHN: Not all, George, just those who get a major chunk of the business like you do. I've seen it before. Give a major share of your buying to one organization and they take advantage of you.

GEORGE: So you don't believe in this partnership idea that was discussed three years ago when the agreement was put together.

JOHN: Partnership! That's bullshit! You guys just threw that term around to get the business, and you have no idea what it means. Six months after we signed the agreement I'm told that Paul [the original salesperson assigned to the account] is being transferred and you show up at my door. Like, "Here's who you're dealing with, take it or leave it." That's no way to treat a partner. Then, on the first big order for the new ZX-190 board, you tell me it's going to take the normal ten to twelve weeks for delivery. When I yell about it, my boss calls your boss and gets it done in four weeks. That makes me look like an idiot. And you tell me you want a partnership!

GEORGE: Whew! We really let you down early on when it was important to create some credibility. First of all, I get dumped in your lap after you had developed a relationship with Paul. Then the ZX-190 screwup happened and you learned that the louder someone yells the more things happen. Right?

JOHN: That's right, George. Unless I stay on your back, I'm worried about what you'll do next.

GEORGE: Okay, so there's three points you've stressed. First of all, you think it's risky to give one supplier a major chunk of your business; second, we did a couple of things early on that let you down and reinforced your concern about being taken advantage of; and finally, we embarrassed you in front of your boss on the ZX-190 project.

JOHN: You got it.

George is now sure that he has heard John correctly, and more importantly, he feels comfortable that John feels heard. Now he can reassert himself and again communicate his problem. His listening to John has set the stage for John to be open to listen to him so he can go into greater detail.

GEORGE: John, I'm sorry those obstacles have come between us. And I want to tell you again that the threats and pressure you put on us don't work for me. They, in fact, sabotage the very thing you say you want. That is, to be able to trust your supplier to deliver quality products at the best possible price.

You see, when you put the heat on, two things happen. First of all, people tune you out. I'm even tired of your flak and I know that nothing we do will make you happy, so why bust my buns. Second, we go into overkill to produce your boards. There's a lot of unnecessary overtime, double- and triple-checking the process, and other expenses which we have to eventually pass along to you. There's a lot of waste in the system, from the communication between you and me to the way our people deal with it, and I'll even bet we'd find some waste on your side due to the uncertainty we've created. So what I'm saying is that what you and I are doing now isn't working.

Notice how George spelled it all out in concrete terms so that John could easily see the impact on him. This could not have happened, however, had George not listened to John and understood his position.

JOHN: So what do you suggest?

GEORGE: Well, let's step back and look at the total picture for a moment. From what I'm hearing, to make sure the relationship works for you, you want (a) to feel comfortable that you're not being taken advantage of, (b) some input into our decisions that affect you all, and (c) quality products at the lowest possible prices. Is there anything else you would add?

JOHN: Look, George, the bottom line is we want reliable products available on the manufacturing line when we need them and at a reasonable price. That's it. And my job is to make sure that happens.

GEORGE: Okay, good.

JOHN: Oh, and I want to stress this point again. When we use you as a single-source supplier of a custom product we are really putting ourselves at risk. There is no backup. When you guys screw up, we have to shut down the line, and that's a costly mistake.

GEORGE: So you've really got your neck stuck out, and I think I'm pretty clear about your position. I want to find a way we can improve the situation and reduce that risk. What I need is three things: one is a happy customer, two is more information like forecasts of your production requirements, and three is accurate data from you that indicates when we're not doing our job.

Look, we're in a partnership here whether you and I like it or not. Now we've got both sides of the issue out on the table. Have you got any ideas that might solve the problem?

That concludes *Step 1: Define the Problem.* Through his listening, George had been able to bring to the surface apparently all of John's needs and feed them back to John to make sure he knows George has heard them. At the same time, George has honestly and succinctly communicated his needs. When done properly, Step 1 may take the longest time of any step in the process. But, that's all right because it's essential to lay a strong foundation for the conflict-resolution process.

Time invested up front will pay dividends down the line. It's now time to go to *Step 2: Generate Possible Solutions.* Notice that George asked John for his ideas first. This shows your respect for the other person and their input and allows you the opportunity to model for them the importance of listening and not evaluating at this time. Furthermore, if they have a solution that also works for you it's better for it to come from them, thereby enhancing their commitment to it.

JOHN: Well, it sounds like we need more and better communications. So perhaps we should have a meeting every week or even a daily phone conversation to discuss what's going on. That way I could keep an eye on you guys.
GEORGE: (smiles and writes down the two proposed solutions on his pad) Okay, does anything else come to mind?

It's a good idea to listen and acknowledge verbally or nonverbally that you noted the solutions and then ask, "Is there anything else?" This makes sure you're not going to just go for the first idea. It's important to make sure all possible solutions come to the surface at this time.

JOHN: Well, not really, except . . .
GEORGE: Sounds like you're hesitant about something.
JOHN: Well, I was thinking about the possibility of developing a form that we could just fax to each other daily to keep each other informed.
GEORGE: Okay, so that's another possibility we could look at.
JOHN: You know, George, what would really work for me is to have a meeting once a month with all the key people on both sides so we get everyone involved and off my back, and then weekly you and I could get together and review the status.

They've identified several options, and now John has proposed one that works for him. He has already gone to *Step 3: Evaluate the Solutions* in his mind. Now it's time for George to add his input.

GEORGE: Actually, John, I really like what I've been hearing. I also think the basis for improving the relationship is to improve the trust level. And the only way to regain that trust is through communication. So I like your ideas. The daily phone calls or faxes could become a burden, so I don't like those ideas as much as a weekly meeting, and I do agree we should get other people in our organizations involved. So it sounds like we're in agreement about a weekly meeting. When do you want to start, and who do you think should be there?

They have now evaluated their alternatives and also completed *Step 4: Decide on a Mutually Acceptable Solution.* George's final question is an invitation to go to *Step 5: Implement the Solution,* which is to determine *who* does *what* by *when.*

JOHN: Well, here's what I suggest. Let's each of us go back to our own people and get some input from them on who should attend the monthly meetings and what the agenda should look like. Then you and I can get together next week and finalize the plan including a discussion on what our weekly meetings should include. How's that sound to you?

GEORGE: It sounds great to me. The only thing I would add is that in ninety days you and I should get together for the specific purpose of evaluating how this is working. Let's make sure that this solution, in fact, solves the core problems between us.

Here George sets up the meeting to complete *Step 6: Evaluate the Results.*

JOHN: Okay, that sounds good to me. Call me on Friday, and we'll set up next week's meeting.

GEORGE: I'll call you Friday, and John, I want you to know that I appreciate your willingness to have this conversation. I feel much better, and I'm more confident that we'll be much more effective now with less stress and tension. Thanks.

Always thank the other person for their cooperation and willingness to work through the issues with you.

This example, of George and John, shows the possibilities that exist in the Synergistic Paradigm. Extraordinary results can happen when you step outside the boundaries of your traditional thinking about conflict, have the courage to try a new approach, and use the skills presented in this book to create new ways of relating to others. Selling today is too complex and challenging to continue to live with the primitive approach to resolving the conflicts between you and your buyer, you and your sales manager, and you and the support functions that impact your success.

Chapter Summary

1. Unresolved conflicts between individuals greatly limit a salesperson's effectiveness and dramatically impact an organization's sales, customer service, and profitability.
2. Most people fear conflict as a result of growing up in a culture based on the traditional win-lose approach to conflict resolution and the subsequent consequences.
3. Conflict is often avoided at all cost. People employ one of two strategies: the "ostrich approach"—avoid it, don't admit it exists, don't talk about the differences or disagreements; or the "I'll do anything to keep peace in the family approach"—do anything to be nice to others and not create problems.
4. The consequences of either strategy are devastating to sales effectiveness.
5. The three guidelines to effective no-lose conflict resolution in the Synergistic Paradigm are
   • accept conflict as a normal part of a relationship;

- commit yourself to no-lose (or win-win) conflict resolutions;
- use the six-step method for finding mutually acceptable solutions.

6. Conflicts are inevitable and serve a healthy function in every relationship. The key is not to avoid or deny conflicts but to learn how to approach and resolve them in a way that actually benefits the relationship.

7. There are three approaches to resolving conflict:
   - Method 1: I Win-You Lose
   - Method 2: I Lose-You Win
   - Method 3: I Win-You Win

8. Both Methods 1 and 2 leave one party a resentful loser with unmet needs, while Method 3 does not harm the relationship and, in fact, improves it.

9. The major benefits of Method 3 are
   - relationships become healthier and more productive;
   - there is an increased commitment to carry out the decision;
   - the decisions are often of a higher quality;
   - decisions are often made more quickly.

10. The six steps of Method 3 are
   - define the problem (in terms of needs, not competing solutions);
   - generate possible solutions;
   - evaluate solutions;
   - decide on a mutually acceptable solution;
   - implement the solution;
   - evaluate the results.

SHAPE YOUR OWN FUTURE

OR BE SHAPED BY IT

Do not follow where the path may lead; go instead where there is no path and leave a trail. —ANONYMOUS

Mastering the skills of the Synergistic Paradigm is a journey. Taking steps toward becoming more competent in building effective relationships with others is a process of consistent practice and continuous growth and of ongoing improvement. As Somerset Maugham said, "Only mediocre people are always at their best."

Now is the time to begin that journey. But you must take the initiative. No one can do it for you. Take the story of Freddy the Frog and his friend.

One afternoon Freddy the Frog was hopping down a dirt path when he heard cries for help coming from the bottom of a rut in the road. A closer inspection revealed another frog stuck in the rut. The frog asked Freddy for help, and without a second thought Freddy jumped into the rut to show his new friend how to get out. Freddy first demonstrated the "double somersault frog-out-of-the-rut jump," and he landed up on the path with great form. After several attempts, however, his friend gave up and said it would never work for him. So back into the rut went Freddy to demonstrate yet another surefire method to get out. This jump, the "half-gainer with a full twist frog-out-of-the-rut jump," again put Freddy out of the rut and up safely on the path. Once again, his new friend tried several times and gave up declaring that it wouldn't work for him. So one more time Freddy went back into the rut and executed a very simple "swan, frog-out-of-the-rut jump." This time his new friend made at least a half-dozen attempts before finally declaring that he was positive that he was stuck in the rut forever and thanking Freddy for his efforts.

A short time later, while resting on his favorite lily pad, Freddy heard someone behind him and turned to see his new friend bouncing down the path as fast as he could. As he came to rest on the adjacent lily pad, Freddy asked him how he finally managed to get out of the rut. His new friend exclaimed, "The wagon was coming!"

Not only is the wagon coming, it's here. It's time to "get out of the rut" of the traditional approach to selling. The game of selling has changed and so have the rules for success. Those individuals and organizations who do not get out of the rut are losing ground daily, and that's nothing compared to what the future will bring. It's really very simple. You will not survive in the new game without learning how to play by the new rules.

It's as if you have been playing football throughout your

career. You and your organization have developed a certain level of success based on the rules of football. You were trained in, or learned on your own, the basics of the game. You know everything from the size and layout of the field, the shape of the ball, and the procedures of play, to how the scoring is handled. Furthermore, you know how to play the game, from blocking and tackling your opponents, to passing, catching, and kicking the football. Your entire organization is built around this sport, and all of the strategies, training, language, and incentives are based on the game of football.

Now assume that one morning you wake up and discover that the entire team was sold to a new individual who owns a major-league baseball franchise. You and your teammates are now playing baseball. Think of the changes that would be required. Everything you know and are familiar with must go. New rules must be learned and new skills developed. And a new culture must evolve to support the game you are now playing—baseball.

That's how dramatic the changes in selling must be. The paradigm shift in selling has created a whole new game. You can wish it hadn't happened, you can hold on to the good old days, you can deny the evidence, and you can resist it all you want. The bottom line is that the factors outlined in chapter 1 demand a new game of selling, and the traditional approach is confining, limiting, and even inadequate. To not be sensitive to these changes is to risk your very survival. History is full of examples of individuals and organizations who failed to survive a paradigm shift because they were unable to adapt to the new rules.

There are many reasons why it is so difficult for individuals as well as organizations to see clearly the need for change. These obstacles actually hamper your ability to effectively gather and analyze the data necessary to look at different ways of doing things. You may, in fact, be personally experiencing one of these barriers now as it relates to the dramatic shift needed in selling. One thing you can be sure of: your organization is experiencing at least one, and probably more, of these obstacles.

PARADIGM BLINDNESS

Remember that our paradigms act as filters through which we look at life, and there is a tendency to distort information to make it fit our paradigms or reject it altogether. We are blind to information that does not fit. To prove this point, we ask participants in our seminars to look around the room and identify everything they can that's blue. They're then told to close their eyes and list everything they saw that's orange. The typical reaction is that they don't remember any orange objects. They were conditioned to look for blue and were, therefore, blind to other possibilities.

Your paradigms work the same way, and your conditioning about selling may blind you from seeing the need for many of the changes demanded by the new paradigm. There will be a tendency for individuals and organizations to discount, or even reject, some of the information in this book. This is especially true for those who have been very successful at the traditional approach to selling. They will have more trouble giving up what's made them successful in the past and risking the change to a new set of rules.

Paradigm blindness makes you a prisoner of your past and limits many new possibilities in your life. Unless your paradigms change, your future becomes very predictable.

BLAMING OTHERS OR OUTSIDE CIRCUMSTANCES

When things don't go right, the natural reaction is to blame the poor results on something else outside of yourself. At the present time, the most popular scapegoat is the economy. In our seminars, salespeople spend a great deal of time explaining why the economy blocks their ability to perform. They also blame the competition, the product design, the quality, the price, poor customer service, their boss, the marketing department, even the government. Organizations use many of the same excuses, or they find a sacrificial lamb, someone in the organization that they can blame for the lack of results.

It's amazing how many times we've seen capable executives terminated when it's actually the system that's broken.

When you quit blaming outside circumstances for your results, you will be more able to clearly see that the traditional paradigm of selling is bankrupt. As a result, you will experience your own power in changing your paradigms and being responsible for your own life. Once you accept that fact, you'll be more motivated to apply the new skills and your results will improve dramatically.

WORKING HARDER

Another obstacle to the paradigm shift is the work-harder mentality. If sales are off, and you work harder, then naturally sales will improve. Not true, when the game has changed. Rather than accepting the fact that the game has changed and learning the new skills required to play in the new game, many salespeople and sales executives simply believe that working harder is the answer. That's the same thing as having the football team practice even harder at football when they are now playing baseball.

Actions in a paradigm that doesn't work don't work. Working harder is similar to increasing the speed of the train. The results will be the same, you'll just get there faster. The track controls the direction of the train, and until you examine the existing track and then lay new track, you'll get the same results. The new game of selling requires that individuals and organizations lay new track.

DENIAL

Still other individuals and organizations will block their transformation by denying that a problem exists. They are simply not willing to address the problems or issues and admit that there may be new ways of improving the situation. Here individuals stubbornly go on their way, afraid that accepting input or coaching from others is a sign of weakness. "I will do it at any cost" is their motto. Many successful salespeople are now in denial about the changes in the market-place. They are stuck in the rut that built their success and afraid of now having to change. Organizations do the same thing when they label someone who brings up problems as "not a team player" or they create a "they shoot the messenger" culture. The message in either case is "Keep your nose to the grindstone and don't bring up problems or issues. Just do your job and don't make waves."

Individuals and organizations in denial are like those people who don't check the oil in their car until the oil light comes on. Well, the oil light is on! Selling today requires a whole new set of skills, and this book is the warning signal.

A revolution has occurred, one that will forever change the way we sell. The revolution has far-reaching implications for individuals and organizations. The standards for success in selling in the future will be established by those who adapt rapidly and effectively to the rules and skills the new game demands. It's time to proactively shape your own environment rather than being shaped by the limitations of the existing one.

A paradigm shift opens up new possibilities. Columbus, in discovering the new world and creating a paradigm shift, opened the door to new opportunities never imagined by the citizens of civilization at that time. Ask an average merchant prior to 1492 about the vast riches, new products, and possible opportunities available in the new world and they could only respond in the context of their current thinking. Most would have been unable to comprehend the possibilities that lay before them. It is difficult for most humans to think beyond the boundaries of their current paradigms.

It's as if you asked a caterpillar about flying. The caterpillar could not describe flight. He would say caterpillars don't fly. They are ground crawlers, and besides that, if God wanted caterpillars to fly, he would have given them wings. So the caterpillar could not even relate to the possibility of flight. Only after a caterpillar has gone through the process of transformation and become a butterfly could he describe what it's like to fly. Butterflies can describe how caterpillars came to fly.

Imagine, for a moment, life as a salesperson in the new paradigm of selling. Consider these possibilities.

You love your job in sales. It provides you an opportunity to make a great income doing something you enjoy. Your work is stimulating, challenging, and a source of great satisfaction in your life. You have a sense of accomplishment and self-confidence, and your pride in what you do is obvious to those around you. Furthermore, this enthusiasm for your work flows into other areas of life. People admire your zest and vitality.

One of the most enjoyable areas of your work is the relationships you have with others. Your customers treat you like a partner in their buying decisions, trusting your advice and input. These relationships with your customers are built on an open flow of honest communication with no hidden agendas, balanced with a care and concern for the other's needs. When problems arise, they are confronted head-on and resolved with both you and your customers respecting each other and appreciating the value of the relationship. Your confidence in building these synergistic relationships makes it easy for you to search for new business as well as follow up on leads and referrals from friends and existing clients.

Your relationships within your organization or those with whom you interact during the selling process are just as strong. Your manager is supportive and understanding yet challenges and empowers you to even higher performance levels. He is your peak-performance coach, and you trust and value his input. The relationship with your manager is a model for the rest of the organization. Other departments support your efforts. The sense of collaboration and teamwork reinforces your personal commitment to customer satisfaction, and every member of the team feels valued for their contribution to the effort.

You are committed to your own personal growth and development. You enjoy discovering new processes for improving your performance and overall satisfaction from life. You eagerly participate in sales-training seminars sponsored by either your organization or outside sources. These programs are stimulating, exciting, and challenging. They not only provide you new tools to enhance your job performance, but also allow you to transfer the skills and concepts to other areas of your life. You have a sense that the training is providing you an opportunity to grow as a well-rounded individual.

You work in an organizational culture committed to customer satisfaction that respects the role salespeople play in that commitment. The team of people you work with have common goals, and yet the team respects the individual contributions of each member. The team is balanced with visionary thinking and practical application. You and your fellow team members share a commitment to quality, to customer satisfaction, and to excellent financial results. You feel as if you are part of a community of people that is making a difference in each other's lives and a contribution to the organization and its customers.

That description is not of heaven, nirvana, or utopia. It shows what's possible in the new paradigm of selling. If it hits you as impossible, that's okay. Remember, caterpillars don't know how to fly. Then consider the words of Mahatma Gandhi: "To believe what has not occurred in history will not occur at all is to argue disbelief in the dignity of man."

Once exposed to the value of this new technology, it will be easy for individuals and organizations to reject the old model. Assume that for some reason call waiting and answering machines or voice mail were no longer available. Think of the frustrations you would experience in getting a busy signal or no answer when calling someone. We have become used to the convenience and efficiency these new technologies provide us. Even these relatively simple technological advances changed our lives forever, and to return to the previous level of technology would seem primitive. The same is true for the new model of selling and its "technology" in this book. Once salespeople have experienced the benefits and personal value from selling with the Sales Effectiveness Training method, they will never return to the "old way" of selling.

Let's now look at each of the cornerstones of the paradigm shift in selling and examine how some individuals and organizations are adapting to the new game and effectively preparing for the future.

THE SELLER-BUYER RELATIONSHIP

If you're not committed to building a dramatically different kind of relationship with your prospective buyers and customers, you simply may not survive in the marketplace. In chapter 1 we examined some of the issues in the business climate of the 1980s and early 1990s that demanded a new model for relationships between buyers and sellers. From conversations with our clients and others, it appears that the future holds more of the same with less room for error and, therefore, even higher stakes.

Michael Bender was the sales training manager for the AC Delco division of General Motors in the late 1980s. He recognized the need for a radical new approach to selling to their distribution network and convinced management to support his beliefs. As a result, he supervised the delivery of our Synergistic Selling and Customer Relations courses to over one thousand people in sales and customer relations positions.

Now an independent consultant in France, he remains committed to the new model of selling. He not only saw the value of the new model to AC Delco but now projects an even more urgent need in the marketplace. Bender says:

> The challenges salespeople face are so varied and considerable that the old planned approaches and canned solutions can lead only to a break in communications, then loss of sales, and ultimately jeopardize the survival of the company. One can say it is a categorical imperative that a prerequisite for salespeople today is training and a strong grounding in the philosophy of the Synergistic Paradigm.

He goes on to emphasize that the volatile business environment also affects the buyer:

One must not forget that the rapidly changing marketplace makes the Buyer as uncomfortable as the Seller, and a lot more suspicious of representatives who continue to use the same old tools of the trade.

Another pioneer in exploring the benefits of the Synergistic Paradigm is Alex Kerr of SaskTel (Saskatchewan Telecommunications). Beginning in 1985, as supervisor of marketing training, he brought the Synergistic Selling course to SaskTel. His objective was to prepare salespeople and others for the competitive marketplace the organization faced with deregulation of the telecommunications industry in Canada. Since that time, over two thousand people throughout the organization have participated in the program. Kerr says:

The marketplace of the nineties is even more competitive than we expected. The key to success lies in the organization's ability to maintain synergistic relationships with its customers. The training we provided our people from 1985 through 1990 simply set the stage. The skills of Synergistic Selling need to be dusted off and constantly reinforced in the culture.

Another who agrees that the future will demand stronger partnerships between buyers and sellers is David Borschelt, director of sales for GMAC in Detroit. In the mid 1980s, Borschelt was part of a team that developed a new position at GMAC branches responsible for enhancing the relationships with General Motors dealers. He and the other team members realized that the traditional approach to selling wouldn't work in the scope of the position they were creating. They used Synergistic Selling to train the new breed of managers in the skills necessary to build and maintain healthier long-term relationships. Borschelt sees an even greater need in the future for these relationship management skills. He says:

> Buyers in every field are going to limit the number of people they do business with and want stronger partnerships with those they do. There will be less and less jumping to the "deal of the day." In other words, pricing will be less of a factor because of a narrower band of pricing resulting from the increased availability of technology among competitors. The relationship will increasingly become a more important factor in buying decisions.

The business challenges of the future will only increase the pressure on the buyer-seller relationship. Let's examine some of the key issues organizations face in the years ahead that will call for constantly improving the relationship between salespeople and their customers.

First is the Total Quality Management movement and its priority of creating a customer-oriented culture. This is not a fad nor is it the management philosophy of the month. TQM represents an evolution to a new way of doing business. W. Edwards Deming, arguably the leading proponent of the quality movement, calls for a metamorphosis, a transformation, in an organization's operating style to effectively survive in the future. This is a gradual process of continuous improvement that is being woven into the very fabric of organizational cultures. It's not going to go away. A vital key to any TQM program is the relationship the salespeople and others build with the customers. Honest and open communication and effective problem-solving skills are essential for salespeople to operate in this environment.

Additionally, the technological complexity of today's products and services demands even longer and more involved relationships between buyers and sellers, and there's no sign of that changing in the future. The same is true for the growing trend toward the customization of products and services. No longer can the salesperson or her organization simply make a sale and move on. The interdependent nature of the relationship between the organizations requires an even stronger bonding. Sellers and buyers will be forced to have a more thorough understanding of each other's companies, and this will require the sharing of information thought to be proprietary before. Buyers are going to be a lot more selective about whom they do business with. The margin of error is shrinking in the competitive marketplace, and mistakes are too costly to take buying decisions lightly.

The trend toward developing single-source partnerships will continue as the technology becomes more complex. Likewise, the development of new products and services with new technologies will further the need for stronger relationships between buyers and sellers.

Finally, the cultural issues predictably inherent in a global marketplace will necessitate closer buyer-seller relationships. Not only will salespeople need to be skilled in managing the customer relationship differently, but they will have to do it in an arena of cultural diversity. Michael Bender is experienced in the impact of cultural differences, having spent ten years in General Motors' European division prior to his AC Delco assignment. He says this about the global marketplace:

> Companies are rushing to position themselves across international borders. The danger is that they have not factored into their plans what it will take to compete successfully in such an environment. Sadly, too many believe that they only have to extend their business-as-usual thinking. This is leading only to disaster because the local customer [in Europe] isn't accepting this approach.

The business-as-usual thinking that Bender refers to is the traditional approach to the seller-buyer relationship. He adds:

> Most cross-cultural selling problems arise not out of disagreement, but out of misunderstandings between

the buyer and seller. This is true when both parties are speaking the same language, and are considered fluent in that language. Sales representatives better get in tune where a multi-cultural situation exists. The pan-European salesperson will have to discard his old methods and move to the Synergistic Paradigm to be successful.

What Bender is saying again is that the globalization of the marketplace calls for a new sense of understanding and collaboration between buyers and sellers.

The issues facing today's organizations and salespeople that have prompted the development of a new kind of buyer-seller relationship are just the tip of the iceberg compared to what we will experience in the future. If you are not already making the necessary changes in your approach to that relationship, you are not in the ball game. If you don't make those changes in the future, you may never get into the game.

THE RELATIONSHIP BETWEEN SALESPEOPLE AND THEIR MANAGERS

Perhaps the area of greatest possible improvement in sales results from the Synergistic Paradigm is the relationship between salespeople and their managers. For most salespeople, this relationship is a source of frustration and resentment. It stifles personal motivation, creativity, enthusiasm, and commitment. Even at best, it seems to be neutral or simply acceptable, not a source of motivation for salespeople to achieve greater results. Rare is the situation when a salesperson describes the relationship with his manager as a positive, empowering partnership.

The message here is simple and straightforward: radical adjustments must be made in the relationship between salespeople and their managers in order to maximize individual and organizational effectiveness. There is no other way to look at it. The transformation must be fundamental and pervasive.

There are several issues to examine. First, the new buyer-seller relationship demands the involvement of individuals who can make decisions. Buyers don't want to deal with an "errand-boy." They want to work with a salesperson who is sufficiently trained to do her job and has the authority to make decisions pertinent to their partnership. Furthermore, the rapidly changing marketplace calls for salespeople with more autonomy. The game demands the decision-making capabilities from those in action on the playing field.

Second, salespeople, like their peers in other areas of the organization, are insisting on a radical new set of values in the workplace. They want more responsibility and greater self-direction. They want to have greater input into the decisions that affect them. Moreover, they want their work to be more rewarding and provide a greater sense of personal accomplishment and contribution to others. The salesperson today, and even more so tomorrow, wants her opinions, attitudes, and beliefs respected and treated with dignity. Sales managers must be able to provide a work environment where those needs can be met.

For most organizations, the typical solution to improving the relationship between salespeople and their managers is empowerment. Empowerment of the sales force is discussed everywhere, in training sessions, at annual sales meetings, and at executive conferences. Yet most "empowerment" is a farce. In most corporate cultures, it appears that empowerment is something that's done to the salesperson. It's another form of control. That's why, to many salespeople, it's just another way for the organization to get them to do what upper management wants them to do. Typical empowerment comes across as subtle control and manipulation.

In our work with sales managers, we ask them to define empowerment. They respond with answers such as "Empowerment is getting salespeople to work harder or to be more productive, to achieve quota, to become more responsible, to solve their own problems, to take more initiative, to learn more so they'll be more effective." The answers all have one common denominator: they represent the manager's agenda. It seems that empowerment is something that you do to another person to get them to do what you think needs to be done. And remember, if the other person doesn't have any input into the process, they will resist it.

Empowerment is, in fact, the key to transforming the salesperson–sales manager relationship that's so critical in today's marketplace and to prepare for the future. However, in the Synergistic Paradigm, enpowerment takes on a new meaning. True empowerment involves creating an environment where individuals are encouraged to work toward the actualization of their capabilities. This includes focusing on the interdependent nature of relationships as well as individual well-being; allowing for self-direction and self-responsibility; and providing an opportunity to examine and alter self-limiting beliefs. The key word here is *interdependent*. An empowering environment is one in which both individuals have a responsibility in its creation.

Our culture places a lot of emphasis on the role of the manager or the leader, yet the "followers" have responsibility also. That's why altering the relationship between salespeople and their managers is not solely the responsibility of the sales manager. A salesperson, too, must assume accountability in transforming the relationship with her manager.

Salespeople have a tendency to abdicate power to their manager and then complain when things don't go right. In fact, followers do that in a lot of different areas. For example, look at how we blame one person, the president of the United States, for the country's economic woes. Followers appoint a leader and then expect the leader to save them, or they wait for a leader to lead them out of their woes. It is easier to give our power to someone else and then blame them for what's wrong than to accept personal responsibility for our own lives. By and large, salespeople fear the authority their boss represents and are far too passive in the relationship. For "empowerment of the sales force" to work, the salespeople must be willing to accept the responsibility that goes along with it.

Likewise, managers must accept their role in altering the relationship. The traditional approach to sales management is obsolete. Sales managers must develop a new set of skills to enhance their effectiveness today. After all, in the purest sense, the role of a manager is to create conditions under which the individual can bring their own capabilities to bear and can tap into their own inner potential and maximize their personal effectiveness. Perhaps the best model to look at is that of a coach.

William Marre, co-founder and former president of the Covey Leadership Institute, is now an independent consultant specializing in developing coaching skills in managers. Marre believes it's important to refine the distinction people have about "coaching." He says:

> The type of coaching that is essential to improve sales performance today is not the directive style most people are familiar with. This is the style used in football, for example, where the coach sits in the pressbox with a broader view of the game and sends in plays. This is not an empowering style. A more successful type of coaching for salespeople today is that used by the tennis coach. The rules of the game actually prevent coaching during the match. Instead, the tennis coach helps prepare the player for the game and then gives feedback on performance.

Marre's coach is one who provides resources and creates conditions for the individual to achieve peak levels of performance. This coaching style allows for the self-direction and self-responsibility that salespeople want. This is true empowerment.

The relationship between salespeople and their managers must be altered to create the sales effectiveness demanded in today's high-pressure business climate. Sales managers must become proficient in their new role of a coach. They must first unlearn much of what they've been taught about management and be willing to adopt new skills. Furthermore, salespeople must also be committed to creating a more productive relationship with their managers. They need to accept personal responsibility for developing an empowering relationship that allows them to maximize their effectiveness.

THE RELATIONSHIPS WITH OTHERS INVOLVED IN THE SELLING-BUYING PROCESS

The increasingly complex marketplace continues to create additional frustration for salespeople. In almost every area of selling, there are more people involved with the selling process. In large organizations, there are typically more people and a more complicated structure of support departments that impact the sales and delivery of quality products and services. Moreover, from entrepreneurs running small businesses to independent real estate or insurance salespeople, there are more people involved with consummating a sale and then servicing the customer.

The future holds more of the same as the trend of breaking down formal lines of authority within an organization continues. Furthermore, the increased movement toward specialization will mean more people and additional business units in the selling and servicing cycle.

Alex Kerr explains: "As our technology grows, there will be a greater need for more interfacing with the customer. From technicians to product design to customer training and support, there will be more people involved with our customers."

Michael Bender makes the same point from a different perspective. He says:

One must not forget that companies moving across international boundaries to achieve growth are not necessarily hiring more people to handle this projected new business. This is resulting in more and more internal "non-sales people" coming in direct contact with the customer. If these people are not trained and committed to the Synergistic Paradigm, the company runs the risk of losing future repeat sales.

The real message is that sales effectiveness today, and probably more so tomorrow, is dependent on the salesperson's ability to coordinate the efforts of many individuals over whom she has no direct authority. She interacts daily with an interdependent network of individuals, each with their own agendas. While they might all agree that they are committed to customer satisfaction, they certainly have different ways of getting the results and even different standards by which to measure the results. Success depends on the salesperson's ability to build and maintain productive partnerships with others who impact her selling process.

The important distinction to make here is the difference between *agreement* and *alignment*. Agreement is a state in which the individuals are in a compatible or harmonious relationship. This usually implies acceptance and accommodation; a lack of discord or conflict. Agreement accepts the status quo because changing something may risk disagreement. This state, therefore, breeds conformity.

Alignment, on the other hand, is a generative act. It is a way of being that brings forces into a straight line, on the same wavelength. It is synergistic in nature. In other words, the results produced are greater than either party would be able to accomplish on their own. Alignment requires confronting the disagreement that typically lies underneath the agreement.

Salespeople typically interact with other individuals, or groups, in a harmonious and compatible relationship only because there is an unspoken agreement not to bring disagreements to the surface. Many times we have worked with clients who told us they had a great team attitude because everyone got along. That alone is a red flag. When we processed the unspoken communication exercise in our course, we discovered tremendous resentment lying below the surface of the relationships. We were then able to resolve the issues and create alignment, and a much more productive team.

The two examples below visually reflect this distinction.

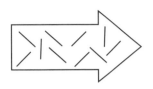

AGREEMENT

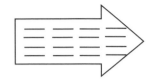

ALIGNMENT

In a relationship with another individual inside, or outside, your organization that impacts your effectiveness in selling, agreement leaves unresolved issues that form a maze that must be transgressed in order to complete your job. You can probably identify three issues right now that you don't agree with that limit your effectiveness. Yet, in order to maintain agreement, you simply find ways to work around them. Many of these obstacles become the "that's just the way it is" reality you adjust to daily.

Four steps are essential to generating alignment with any individual or groups of individuals that impact your sales effectiveness:

1. Have a clear sense of the vision, the commitment to sales results, and excellent customer satisfaction.
2. Do not accept the status quo, the normal way of doing things. Be willing to explore new possibilities and greater levels of personal and organizational effectiveness.
3. Be authentic in your communication. Speak the truth and be committed to confronting the "sacred cows" that are limiting your success.
4. Resolve the issues that surface with a commitment to win-win outcomes.

The challenges that face salespeople today, including the importance of customer satisfaction, the competitive nature of the marketplace, the need for rapid responses to customer needs, the technology, and the impact of globalization, insist on a new sense of collaboration. Simple agreement is no longer acceptable.

Alignment with others yields the level of personal effectiveness and organizational efficiency necessary for survival in the years ahead.

SALES TRAINING

Attention Sales Managers and Other Executives: If you don't commit yourself to training and developing your personnel today, there's a good chance someone else will be sitting in your chair tomorrow.

Attention Salespeople: If you don't commit yourself to ongoing personal development, whether your organization provides it or not, you probably will not achieve your present level of results in the future.

Training can no longer be considered a nice thing to do when the time and money exist. The development of one's capabilities is essential for survival. The technological complexity, speed of change, and competitive nature of the marketplace insist that training and development become a priority for both individuals and organizations.

In the marketplace of today and even more so tomorrow, companies cannot compete on price or technological advantages. The basis for remaining competitive is the relationships salespeople and others build with their customers and the quality of the service they provide. When you compete on service, people become the vital component. When people matter, training is essential. It is no longer a question of whether to train salespeople or not. Effective training is the prerequisite for survival.

In the agricultural economy of the past, success was measured in the ability to take the raw materials of seeds and harvest crops. Later, in the industrial economy, it was essential to effectively take raw materials and manufacture products. Now, in the service economy, the competitive advantage comes from taking the raw materials, the inner capabilities of human beings, and producing greater personal and organizational effectiveness. No longer is the benchmark of success the yield of the harvested fields, or the number of products manufactured. Today success is measured by the quality of human relationships inside and outside the organization.

Sales performance and customer satisfaction are directly dependent on the effectiveness of relationships with customers and those inside the organization that impact the selling and delivery of quality products and services. The complexity of relationships in today's business environment makes the exploration of human interdependence the next frontier in organizational effectiveness. Those who don't adapt to the new rules and appropriate skills will find themselves left in the dust like those who did not keep up with the technological advances of the last two decades.

These challenges require a new distinction in training. The traditional approach to training salespeople is to identify a deficiency and provide tips and techniques that help the person improve in that area. This type of training, which we call performance-based training, enhances the performance within a given paradigm. It does not usually, however, stimulate people to alter their paradigms and open the door to breakthroughs in performance. While it may produce behavior changes, these changes are typically incorporated within the context of existing beliefs. At best, this training results in incremental behavior improvement.

Transformational training, on the other hand, alters the paradigm from which the individual operates. It allows individuals to move beyond the invisible limitations of existing paradigms and, therefore, has a significant impact on their performance. Training of this nature usually has three main components. First, it provides participants an opportunity to examine their existing paradigms. As a result, they are able to understand the boundaries and the consequences of those boundaries their paradigms create. This is an essential step for people to move beyond the limitations of their past conditioning. Second, transformational training allows individuals to design new paradigms that call for different patterns of behavior that may facilitate a quantum leap in performance improvement. Finally, the training must provide the skills necessary to develop the new behavior patterns.

This new distinction in training allows people to proactively generate new ways of thinking and behaving outside their current context. Rather than learning techniques to enhance a certain behavior, participants in transformational training get to explore different behaviors that may be more effective under the existing circumstances.

Typically, our behavior in any given situation is influenced by our conditioning from similar situations in our past. This limits us to a future that is simply an extension of our past. Transformational training enables individuals and organizations to break out of the limitations of previous conditioning and discover new possibilities.

Here's an example to drive home this distinction. Baby elephants in the circus are tied to a stake driven into the ground. Since they are not strong enough to pull the stake out of the ground, they quickly learn that their movement is restricted to the length of the rope. They are conditioned to believe that's as far as they can go. Adult elephants are, therefore, controlled by being tied to a stake; even though they could easily pull the stake from the ground and walk away, they don't. They are conditioned as babies to believe they aren't strong enough. Our past conditioning, our paradigms, do exactly the same to us.

Traditional performance-based training teaches people how to be more effective within the confines of their existing world as they know it—in other words, within the limits of the length of rope they have tying them to the stake. Transformational training tests their beliefs and their conditioning and allows individuals to move beyond the preconditioned limits of their past experience.

The complexities of today's business environment demand transformational training to more effectively prepare individuals and organizations for the challenges they face. It's no longer acceptable to send salespeople to work without proper training. The question is what training will maximize the results.

The Synergistic Paradigm of selling represents a new game with a new set of rules. The marketplace has created the new paradigm for us. We are now playing baseball with a football mentality, and everyone on the team needs training in the new skills. Conventional performance-based training, improving blocking and tackling, is not appropriate. Only transformational training that allows individuals to shift their thinking from football to baseball and then provides them the skills to play baseball will work.

Not only do salespeople need training in the skills of creating synergistic relationships, but everyone else from top management through clerical support staffs must also be trained in the new model. This is an essential ingredient in the culture shift needed to facilitate the transformation.

It will not happen overnight. The shift must also include constant reinforcement of the synergistic skills and ongoing coaching for continuous improvement. To work effectively in the Synergistic Paradigm requires that people unlearn much of what they have learned in the past. Salespeople have been conditioned to behave in certain ways to be successful in the traditional model. Now the carpet has been pulled out from under them. The dramatic changes that are now necessary require taking risks, being uncomfortable, and breaking through the fears inherent in transformation. This accentuates the need for managers to shift their role to that of coach.

Finally, to effectively prepare salespeople for the marketplace, the training function needs to be more aligned with the rest of the sales organization. Deborah Twadell, vice president of corporate development for Mortgage Guaranty Insurance Corporation and the current president of the National Society of Sales Training Executives, says it this way: